Sensitive? Who wants to be sensitive? There are too many touchy people in this world already!

BUT WAIT! You don't know all the exciting ideas *sensitive* includes! To be *sensitive* is to feel, know, and enjoy completely the messages from your senses—touch, taste, smell, hearing, and sight—to reverberate the excitement of life going on around you.

To be *sensitive* is to respond to the attitudes, feelings, and life-style of others—to belong and really care—that's true love in its best expression.

To be *sensitive* is to be totally aware that you perceive even the slightest changes and differences in the happenings that make your life rich.

To be *sensitive* is to draw people to you; to be nice to be near.

Isn't it interesting that a word with so much warmth and happiness locked in its meaning can be recalled for its lesser connotation! Fortunately for us, this exquisite word has come into its own. Unlock its joys and make them your own. *The Sensitive Woman* will help you do just that!

Sandra S. Chandler decided to write this book because she felt the other books on women and sex missed the mark: the secular how-to-become-sexy types were all flesh and no spirit; the spiritual books were too heavenly to be much earthly good. So the outline for the *Sensitive Woman* was born.

The author draws from a deep reservoir of personal experience. She has counseled scores of women of all ages who have opened their hearts to her. The wife of a journalist who was a pastor for eight years, Sandie has been a choir director and Bible-study leader, an elementary-school teacher, and a speaker to women's groups. She holds a BS degree in education and has taken graduate work in psychology. She and her husband are the parents of Heather, Holly and Timothy.

The Sensitive Woman

SANDRA S. CHANDLER

Compass Press • Pasadena, California
"Publications that point The Way"

First Printing, June, 1972
Second Printing, May, 1973
Third Printing, August 1974

Library of Congress
Catalog Card Number: 75-178885

TO RUSS
My inspiration, lover and husband

CONTENTS

About The Book

This is a book for and about the modern woman. Because of pressures and conflicts she faces in today's troubled society, a woman finds herself in new roles with a greater need to understand men. Many women—and men, too—aren't satisfied with life. Especially with their sex life. This book tells you how to achieve a new awareness through sensitivity and how sensitivity can help you understand yourself, your friends, and most important of all, your lover. I believe sex should bring more than personal gratification; it is the uniting of two bodies, minds, and spirits. Sex must include love if it is to truly satisfy. God must govern love if it is to endure.

This book developed out of my experiences with many women as they shared with me in conversations about their intimate lives and from my desire to help other women become sensitive, sexy, and spiritual. This book is an adventure in learning and loving. It dares you to be a sensitive woman!

—Sandra S. Chandler

ACKNOWLEDGMENTS

Appreciation to Russell May, M.D., of Fairfax, Virginia, for reading the manuscript and giving medical advice.

Quotation of Doctor Perls courtesy of *Harper's* BAZAAR. From "Encounter Games: A Dangerous New Trend," by Bettie Wysor. June, 1971, pages 60, 61. © 1971, by the Hearst Corporation, New York, New York. Used by permission.

Quotation from *Magazine of Modern Sex:* "Swap Clubs and the Law," by William Breedlove. September, 1964, page 124. Printed by Shelbourne Press, Los Angeles, California. Used by permission.

Quotation from *Better Is Your Love Than Wine,* by Jean Banyolak and Ingrid Trobisch. © 1971 by Editions Trobisch, D-757, Baden-Baden, Germany. Used by permission of Inter-Varsity Press, Downers Grove, Illinois.

Quotaton from song, *For All We Know.* © 1970, by Pamco Music, Inc. Los Angeles, California. Used by permission.

Quotation from *The New Testament in Modern English,* by J. B. Phillips. © 1958 by J. B. Phillips. The Macmillan Company. New York, New York. Used by permission.

1

SENSITIVITY AND YOU

A lot of women, when they are only unzipped, think they have been liberated. Deep down, though, I think they know they are really not.

Lately we have had a spate of books and articles on sensual women, and men, and couples. One of these days somebody is bound to write a book about the whole Sensuous Family.

This book is about why so many of the "now" girls and women are not really liberated at all—whether or not they can shed their clothes and their inhibitions. Women are hungry—in fact starving—to know how to be truly liberated. To be fulfilled as women.

You may think this is an extension of a best-seller on how to become a sensuous woman. It isn't. It's more. Much more. Sexuality cannot be condensed into the simplistic notion that to achieve exquisite ecstasy all you have to do is have perfect orgasms—never mind how or with whom.

I have read the books on sex too. Some of the mechanics suggested are fine, but there is more to being a *sensitive* woman than being sexually proficient. Sensitivity can lead to an intensity of physical enjoyment most women have never known.

A sensitive woman is one who is aware of her own needs, drives, and desires; but she is able to go beyond herself. She senses many of the same needs, drives, and desires in persons around her, male and female, young and old. It is exhilarating to be a woman.

Better yet, to be a *sensitive* woman.

In the beginning . . . the universe burst into being at God's command and the earth was hurled into orbit. God created man, but man was not satisfied. He was lonely.

God saw man's need and created woman. She was a beauty and a delight. She was precious and pure.

What contentment! Alone in the garden beside the rippling stream with luscious fruit, bright flowers, and shade-giving trees. Everything a couple could ask for!

So you would think.

But then . . . an evil creature sidled up to woman. He tempted her to eat the fruit of the tree of Knowledge.

She ate it.

This was her big mistake—and the genesis of sin.

Remember that. It should be the number one object lesson to you about your sensitivity to man. They did not discuss the consequences of disobeying God. There was no dialogue, no communication. It was the first—but not the last—time for woman to be beguiled by smooth talk!

The story goes on. It tells about how man and woman became aware of each other. Their eyes were opened. Now they knew good and evil—and the possibility for exploiting one another.

"Games people play" began in the garden. Sex lost its purity. Each saw his mate as an object of satisfaction, not as a person.

The Bible says it all: "They knew that they were naked; and they sewed fig leaves together, and made themselves aprons" (Genesis 3: 7, ASV). They were embarrassed by the naked truth of their sinfulness, and they quickly stitched a cover-up.

If woman had been sensitive to man, and to the evil that could befall her, sin might never have happened. But she wasn't. And it did. So it's your job and mine to be that sensitive woman.

* * *

Change is the order of the day in our world and women—like it or not—are forced to live in these daily changes. They must be sensitively tuned to cope with the change about them.

Consider, if you will, the choices you have to make in today's world that your counterpart of a few decades ago did not have to struggle within her world.

Do you want to be a career woman? If so, are you to be the "liberated" variety? How will you fight for your rights? Or will you be satisfied as you are, believing that you are receiving full rewards for your efforts?

Do you want to be a full-time homemaker? Will you be content to dust the shelves, wash the dishes, wash and iron the clothes, and cook delectable meals? Do you find it a pleasure to entertain friends and those who need someone who cares?

What about being a mother? Will you or won't you? There are the pregnancies, early-morning feedings, doctor visits, breathlessly watching those first steps, seeing the wonder in your child's eyes—all of this and more—versus the freedom to come and go without responsibilities and demands of little ones.

These are just a few of women's roles. You may read this today, and by tomorrow discover the role you chose has changed—or is in the process of changing. No matter what your current choice or circumstance, you must accept or reject what change may bring to your future. You will need to be sensitive to your changing needs.

Begin to think about your life and some of the little things that bother you. Be as honest with yourself as you know how.

Take a few moments now to ask yourself these questions:

1. What are the happiest moments of my life?

2. Do these moments involve anyone else? If so, who? Why?

3. When do I feel most frustrated? Why do I get that way?

4. What is the condition of my health?

5. Do I have any long-range goals? (List several, if possible.) How have I attempted to reach each one?

After you write down your answers, tuck them away. When you have finished reading this book, wait a week or two, then answer the questions again and compare your answers with your first list. If you have followed my suggestions, you should notice a change.

But you are asking: "What does this have to do with sensitivity? All I want is a better sex life and, perhaps, to feel that I am useful to others. I want to be more aware of the needs of others. What will make those around me happier"

Sensitivity can lead to physical pleasure and mutual gratification of high intensity. God intended this kind of sexual fulfillment between lovers. (Speaking about lovers, I'm talking about husband and wife.) But single, divorced, and widowed women have needs too. Sensitive women understand their own needs, drives, and desires of others around them. They know how to fulfill these needs.

The important thing in becoming sensitive is that you seek that greater life of fulfillment.

I speak from experience because I am also on the sensitivity road. I am traveling with a wonderful companion. In fact, two companions—my lover, and God.

I may not arrive at my destination right away. But I'm working on it. And making progress.

You can too!

2

SENSITIVITY DEFINED

Before I can share with you what I have learned in my adventure on the sensitivity road, I need to know that we share a common definition of what sensitivity is. To be sensitive, as I use it, is to be able to respond.

I can already feel how eager you are to know how you can reach your ultimate in sensitivity.

Sensitivity Groups

You may think this book will be about sensitivity groups or "human potential" training. These subjects are related to the ideas in this book but involve only a small part of the total picture of sensitivity.

Sensitivity groups are variously known in today's jargon as humanistic psychology, group dynamics, human potential therapy, Gestalt, awareness, and encouter or "T" groups.

Esalen, one of the first sensitivity groups to receive widespread publicity, came into being in San Francisco in the mid-1960s. Therapy groups like it have since spread throughout the United States. The sensitivity-group movement reaches both sexes and all ages. There are groups meeting in churches, factories, and schools in this country and abroad.

Sensitivity retreats are becoming common throughout the United States. Most sensitivity retreats have a basic theme: building up trust and communication. Participants experience opportunities to release suppressed feelings of anger, fear, pain, hostility, and love. The sessions are devoted to learning by doing. Much of the communication is non-verbal.

My husband attended a church-led sensitivity session. The large group was broken into groups of six. Each group was (without words) to decide which one of the six would pretend to be "seriously injured" while on a mountain hike.

The accident was to be acted out, then the other five were to respond appropriately (all without words), give the "injured" teammate first aid, and assist him back to camp.

Another exercise followed. With eyes closed, everyone in the room was to stretch out his arms and hands at shoulder height and slowly walk about, communicating by feeling each person he touched.

That session, typical of milder sensitivity exercises was devoted to loosening up a conventional group of adults by having them perform simple tasks that require cooperation and basic trust between participants.

Other groups, like Esalen, are overtly sexual in orientation; they are based on a sense of immediacy, and are geared to intense emotional experiences. In fact, intimate responses. The sensitivity-group approach is simple, but for some the outcome can be literally fatal.

In a magazine article, "Encounter Games: A Dangerous New Trend" (June, 1971, *Harper's Bazaar*, pp. 60-61, used with permission) a group-therapy specialist says party encounter games are popular (as are movies such as *Bob and Carol and Ted and Alice* that feature nudity and sensitivity sessions for couples) because they hold out the allure of personal revitalization.

Under proper supervision, the psychologist says, they can be good in a therapeutic sense. Honesty and openness can be encouraged.

People with healthy egos can generally survive— and often benefit— from encounter groups. *But for those who function on a fine line of stability, stripping away natural defense mechanisms may prove too hot to handle.*

Severe psychosis can be triggered by the breakdown of defenses, expression of hostilities, and the concurrent removal of inhibitions.

All too often people who become encounter-group regulars substitute the experiences in the group for real friendship and intimacy.

"It is a kind of programmed intimacy," the psychologist points out. "They go through the motions and maybe they experience something, but it is seldom lasting . . . The danger is that the outcome is often unpredictable, and psychotic episodes can happen."

Sensitivity groups tend to attract unstable and emotionally insecure people. That is not to say, of course, that everyone who attends fits this category.

After going through a series of sensitivity sessions some people encounter "re-entry" problems. Some become unable to live with their spouses. Others can not adjust to their office staff any longer. A common problem is that some T-group enthusiasts seem unable to relate unless they are with those who helped them "release."

Tom is an example. He always held his emotions tightly inside himself; he came away from a series of T sessions holding his mouth open whenever he felt tense. This is how he learned to turn loose of his emotions. When he was at home or at work and would hold his mouth open, he would get the comment, "What's the matter, Tom? Can't you breathe through your nose?"

In many cases, however, sensitivity groups succeed in redefining and enriching the spirit of man. Men and women often come to the groups lonely and hungry for a greater understanding of themselves, and find what they seek.

Sensitivity training has been criticized by some as Communist brainwashing. Most of it is not. The real concern, however, is that many T groups attempt to substitute humanistic psychology for sensitivity of spirit that is essential to our fulfillment as women.

As psychologists and therapists have observed, sensitivity-group benefits have been short lived for many participants. You do not seek the short-lived sensitivity of the group experience alone, but rather the fulfilling sensitivity of the spirit.

Psychic Sensitivity

The word "sensitive," as a noun, is sometimes used to describe a spiritualist, medium, or person endowed with psychic powers. One of the most famous "sensitives" or clairvoyants in recent times was the late Arthur Ford, the medium who purportedly brought messages from the dead son of the late Episcopal bishop, James A. Pike, to the boy's father.

One should not confuse the sensitivity we are discussing in this book with so-called prophetic powers. Sensitivity to the spirit world might be related, but it is not central to our explorations of sexual and spiritual sensitivity.

Sensitivity and Its Responses

In the next chapter, there are some sensitivity exercises that will deal with the responses of the five senses—hearing, seeing, tasting, touching and smelling. There are some other common types of sensitivity as well.

One of the easiest forms of sensitivity to identify

is emotional response. Some of you have experienced emotional sensitivity, or empathy, many times. You have an innate ability to step into someone else's shoes—to feel what they feel.

Remember how you felt when you saw an older person trembling as he hobbled along with a cane; or when your neighbor was depressed after her son was in an auto accident; or when a curly-haired child cuddled a teddy bear to her heart wishing it would return her love?

Can you sense it when someone is becoming temperamental? (I hope you are sensitive to your own temperamental moods so you can bannish—or at least minimize—them.)

Can you sense exuberance, happiness, excitement, and sexual desire? And fear, doubt, self-accusation? When you are in the presense of a friend can you tell if tears (of joy or of sorrow) are just under the surface? And that one wrong—or right—word could set her off into a good cry?

Have you ever been alone after being sick when you have felt very weak and all you could think about was having something cold to drink?

A sense of dryness in the throat and mouth has come to all of us, especially after a bout with the intestinal flu, or working on the lawn on a hot day.

To be able to remember your sensation of thirst is to be sensitive to the physical needs of your neighbor—or your lover.

Another sensitivity is instinctive reasoning or judgment. Many call it woman's intuition. Most women claim to have it, but it needs to be sensitized to be an effective guide to action.

Mrs. Howard, who had a dental appointment at 10:30 one morning, stopped by Mrs. Bryant's house at 9:30. She wanted to see how Mrs. Bryant was getting along after surgery. The two women had a nice chat.

About ten minutes before time to leave for the dentist, Mrs. Howard noticed that Mrs. Bryant's eyes looked strange. Mrs. Bryant continued to talk about how well she felt, but for some reason her friend could not leave.

At 10:30, Mrs. Bryant lost consciousness. Mrs. Howard missed her appointment—and undoubtedly annoyed her dentist. But because Mrs. Howard was sensitive to her friend, she remained and was able to call an ambulance. Her alertness saved Mrs. Bryant's life.

Call it instinctive reasoning, "X-ray eyes" or luck, Mrs. Howard has an uncanny sense that helps her in playing games. Not only does she catch on to new ones quickly, but her friend's chagrin, she usually wins.

Is this luck, talent, or an instinctive comprehension? It may be some of all three. Her instinctive judgment is a refined sensitivity and awareness as well as a natural aptitude or knack.

A similar kind of perception is an intuitive feeling that is not based on anything visible. It is a realization or a discernment about something or someone.

Have you ever known someone very well who was planning to go on a trip, and you feared for his safety? If you are tuned in (sensitive) to him, you will be able to tell him without embarrassment your thoughts.

Some persons seem to have a gift for this type of precognition. Especially between husband and wife, a closeness of spirit sometimes is developed so that one instinctively seems to know when the other is in danger or trouble though they may be thousands of miles apart at the time.

A third sensitivity is the power to perceive direction.

Mr. and Mrs. Gentry went on a camping trip. Mr. Gentry knew exactly where he was at all times when he was in the wilderness, but put him in a big city and he invariably got lost. On the other hand, Mrs. Gentry had only the faintest idea where she was in the wilderness, but she instinctively knew directions in the city and suburbs. In fact, she usually knew the shortest distance between two points while Mr. Gentry wandered around, often taking the most circuitous route!

Aesthetic perception is still another sensitivity. Persons who are sensitive in this area have a keen understanding of and feeling for nature, the arts, and/or music.

Not all persons with artistic or musical sensitivity are talented in the fields. Those who are, though, have sensitivity. An awareness, appreciation, and perception of beauty, form, and character make you sensitive to aesthetic whether or not you can play an instrument or paint a portrait.

Several of the sensitivity exercises in the next chapter will help you develop aesthetic perception by use of the senses.

One example will illustrate how sensitivity to nature can be honed. My husband has kept bees as a hobby since he was a small boy. He has studied these amazing insects carefully and knows all about their habits.

He is sensitive to their presence. Several times when he and I have been out on a hike he has suddenly stood still for a moment, looking up into the sky.

"There's a bee tree nearby," he says.

Sure enough, within minutes he will be standing at the base of a tree. Bees will be going in and out of a hollow in the trunk or a limb.

He is sensitive to the faint buzzing overhead as

well as to the flight patterns when the bees, returning from nectar gathering, converge toward their home.

Until I learned to be sensitive to beelines, I would walk the same route a dozen times without once noticing the winged emissaries overhead.

A final example of sensitivity is "hearing" in silence. Hearing is in quotes because it is not necessarily based on audible sounds. The communication comes through what some counselors call "the third ear."

This has nothing to do with the touch or stare techniques of some sensitivity groups, either.

In the context of what a person says, what he does *not* say is often an important index to the real person. Be alert to what silence says during conversation.

God often speaks to us in stillness when we momentarily muffle the noisy world around long enough to listen to Him.

"Be still and know that I am God," said the Psalmist. After the earthquake, wind, and fire, the "still small voice" brought revelation and comfort to the prophet Elijah.

Sensitivity of the spirit—so essential to our fulfillment as women—comes only through a transforming encounter with God's Holy Spirit.

3

YOU CAN BE SENSITIVE TOO

Did you know your sensitivity can be sharpened through practice?

Webster's dictionary says that the purpose of an exercise is "exertion for the sake of training or improvement, whether physical, intellectual, or moral."

I propose to give you some sensitivity exercises to try. Each is designed to help you become more aware of yourself and your surroundings through the use of five senses. You will become aware of the person next to you, the car coming up the street, the breeze blowing across your face, the tart taste of a lemon, the fragrant apple blossoms of spring.

You may wish to do some of the exercises with someone else.

While these exercises are primarily to develop your sensitivity, and hopefully that of your spouse, they are also excellent for the entire family. Our children learned that parents can grow too.

If you get the ingredients together, you should not have any trouble moving from one exercise to the next. Relax and enjoy doing each one.

Some exercises may sound unnecessary or point-less, but give them a try. They are actually fun! And they are worth the little time they take.

Responding to the Senses

You use your five senses every day. Have you thought about how often you need each one? Try making a little worksheet. Note the senses you use, what you use them for, and what they tell you. The mere exercise of making such a list will cause you to become more aware of the world around you. Your worksheet might look something like this

SENSE	OBJECT	RESPONSE
Sight	mountain lake	clear, relaxing, calm
Smell	mountain lake	pine trees, woodsy
Hearing	mountain lake	lapping water
Touch	mountain lake	cool, refreshing
Taste	mountain lake	bracing, pure—brings back childhood memories

The more sensitive you become, the more you will be aware of the messages from all your senses.

Sight

Seeing is believing, but how much do we really see? A good exercise to help sharpen up this sense is to practice mentally noting objects on a table, in a picture, or in a room. Find a notebook and pencil for yourself, and have someone assemble a collection of items on a table; or visit a model home, art gallery, museum, or other place where the surroundings are not as familiar to you they are in your home. Allow yourself a few minutes to visually examine the objects, a picture, or room, then leave the scene and write down every item you can remember. When you finish you may return to the scene and see how you did on your recall.

How did you feel about what you saw? Keep your comments in your notebook. In a week or so repeat the exercise. Compare your memory and feelings with the first time. Do this periodically and watch your ability to see what you look at improve.

Hearing

An exercise to increase your sense of hearing is to listen to a record and take notes on the lyrics or the instruments used in the orchestra. Just as above, repeat this exercise in a week or so. Concentrate on discriminative hearing.

Another experiment with hearing is to listen to and then record on paper, sounds you hear in the city, home, market, church, park, and of children at play. Write in your notebook the sound you heard, where it was, and how you felt about it. You will be amazed at how quickly your sensitivity to sounds increases.

Smell

Smelling may be less useful than the other senses to your sensitivity development, but these exercises can help you become more aware of the smells in your surroundings—pleasant and unpleasant. While doing the exercise on smell I discovered some familiar odors, but I could not immediately give their sources. This showed me how much I take for granted.

Take a leisurely walk, concentrate on the messages you receive from your nose, and write down the types of smells you notice. Good places to visit include a bakery, fish market, florist, department store, candy shop, popcorn counter—compare the differences. Whether you are driving, or cooking or whatever, you will notice odors. For instance, twenty minutes after you put a pan of brownies in the oven you will begin to smell the aroma. Mmm! Do they smell good! The episode might also remind you of a special time of baking with your mother.

Another experiment (and this must be done with someone else) is to gather together a number of household items with odors. Close your eyes and have your helper test you to see which items you can correctly guess.

Some suggested items to test yourself will include: floor wax, deodorant, shampoo, household bleach, ammonia, perfume, tooth paste, scented candle, various spices, Play-doh, various food stuffs, shaving cream, gasoline, bug spray, camphor. Be careful not to inhale too deeply since some odors are not particularly pleasant or good for the nose in large doses.

After guessing the smells try to remember how you reacted to them. Were they pleasing, nauseating, aggravating, or neutral?

Taste

Similar exercises can be done with taste. You might include your husband, boyfriend, or family members in this. (It could be the beginning of someone special becoming more sensitive.)

You might begin your tasting with the fresh brownies you just baked!

As you taste different things identify each and make notes of whether it is sweet, sour, dry, acid, etc. Do not use the same tastes for both you and your partner. It works best if you each select tastes for the other. Label the items to be tasted—and make sure they are non-poisonous.

Touch

The fifth sense is touch. Collect seven small stones. They must all be different, but similar. Mark them for identification.

Each day take a different stone. Close your eyes. Feel it carefully. Get to know it. Try to describe it. Give it a name.

A week later pick up each stone and recall your original feelings about it. You should remember at least six of the seven stones by name and characteristics you feel.

This exercise may well take the most time and concentration. Most of us are inclined to think that when we have felt one rock we have felt them all. Each rock must become to you something unique, an entity with its own personality.

If you can learn this much about a stone, how exciting it will be when you know your lover that well.

Contemplation

The next sensitivity exercise is very personal: *knowing yourself better through contemplation*. Take your notebook and pencil and find a quiet place.

There are three areas for you to honestly consider. After writing answers to the questions and doing your review work in your notebook, write a paragraph telling about any other thoughts that came to your mind. This will be your personal measuring stick. Be sure to write down every thought and feeling.

The first sequence of questions deals with your background—the years that established the foundation of your life.

1. At what time in history were you born?

2. What were your parents like?

3. Did you have any conflicts? With parents? Friends? Siblings? What kind of conflicts?

4. What were some of your childhood dreams or desires?

5. Have any come true?

Next, think about who you are. Unless you have taken a course in basic psychology you may never have thought about yourself in the following ways. Answer these questions too.

1. How do you conceive of yourself? What qualities do you possess? What hangups do you have?

2. Do you like yourself?

3. How do you think others see you?

4. How would you like others to see you? Make a list.

In your search for sensitivity, you are continually in the process of changing. You are more aware of people, places, and things today than you were yesterday.

You have embarked on a quest for total fulfillment, and you will reach your destination as you understand yourself and your Creator.

There was more to your conception and birth than the union of a man and woman. As a final part of this exercise, review the stages of development of an embryo: the growth of arms, legs, facial features, brain. Review Psalm 139. There is purpose to creation. God has a plan for you. Your awareness of Him and His power of creation is the beginning of a fuller life—especially when you relate this awareness to your personal being.

4

SENSING NEEDS AND CONFLICTS

Why is it you never seem to have the time—or the energy—to create a beautiful love affair? To take off on an impromptu adventure with a friend? To carry on a complete conversation with a child?

Women have more luxuries and commodities within easy grasp of their lotion-smoothed hands than ever before, yet they seem busier than ever.

Some women's lives have become entwined with the telephone and the TV, cosmetics and the hairdresser. Cocktail and bridge parties, the theater and club-work command their time. Then there is chauffering the children to and from their club meetings and private lessons. They have classes to attend and lessons to prepare.

In the midst of busy schedules we hardly have time (or so we think) to explore personality differences, talk about finances or sex with our lovers, or tend to the myriad other little things that spell satisfaction with life. When we do, we only have a few minutes. Or we are exhausted. Or it is the wrong time.

Ever try to discuss money matters when the check book will not balance or when there is too much month left over at the end of the money?

Have you hassled over sex at 3 A.M., after something less than the ultimate intimacy?

Life is too short to be running here and there, never achieving what God wants you to have.

If you really want to be the sensitive woman, put aside everything else for a moment now and concentrate on your own needs and conflicts.

On Needs

Think about your needs first. It probably hasn't been too long since you said, "If only I had more time."

Take time. You deserve the few moments it takes to discover your needs. List them on a piece of paper or the back page of this book.

Affection

I have found that all women need affection. Not necessarily physical affection, although that is essential too. Loving and caressing your lover does bring satisfaction to you as well. But we also need to be loved by our families and close friends.

Knowing this, go beyond yourself to your loved ones. Be sensitive to their needs for love and affection. In correspondence, don't be afraid to begin, "My Dear . . ." In loving, one is loved.

An Exercise to Do: Make a list of any friends or relatives you owe letters. Find a piece of your prettiest note paper and write one person on your list a newsy letter that says by its tone that you are interested in the one to whom you write. Now schedule time each day to write one letter until you have written everyone on your list an affectionate letter.

Tensions and Emotions

Who needs tensions and emotions? We all do. We need to channel emotional energy creatively.

It's good to be emotional when it enables you to vent healthy feelings that need to be expressed. It is bad when it drives you to tears and irrational behavior. I am not against tears—except when they become liquid lachrymal levers to get your own way.

Likewise, tensions are useful when your body is being called upon to meet a crisis. Tension is destructive when it leads to a headache or some other physical discomfort.

According to a Public Health Service survey, singles suffer less nervousness than married people. They have less fear of nervous breakdown and feel less dizziness. They have fewer headaches and heart palpitations.

Companionship

The single woman is likely to have the greatest need for companionship. I have known many college-career age women as well as divorcees and widows who have said, "If only I had a close companion." Your girl friend from college calls and shares all about her marriage. It's great hearing about it, but you yearn for the same type of experience.

You miss the family relationship at home, yet you want and need your independence. Or you think about the good times you shared with your lover or your last boyfriend. At times you wonder if your life will always be this way—you wishing for companionship.

Your loneliness will begin to fade away if you take positive action. You have already begun to change because you are searching. God has a wonderful plan for your life; stay tuned to Him.

What are you doing to make others know you are seeking their friendship? The key lies with you. If you can accept your present condition, knowing that God will be able to mold you according to His will, that should help immensely.

Jesus Christ was a single. He knew periods of

loneliness. What better person to turn to than One who knows?

An Exercise to Do: Look through your local newspaper or telephone book and note announcements of various community organizations that are active. Choose one, and call to find out how you can become a member. Some organizations you might look for include: Parents Without Partners, Community Theater, Community Orchestra, Vocal groups, Writers Guild, Weight Watchers, Newcomer's Club.

Or call a friend you enjoy and plan an impromptu excursion you would both enjoy.

I am only considering a few general needs felt by women. Yours will go beyond those mentioned here. You must discover your own special needs.

Ability to Accept Change

During the middle years there are pressures on a woman that can threaten to tear apart even a well-laminated home. Two bugaboos are menopause and the departure of children.

If you need emotional help—and it often is needed—to clear these hurdles, don't put off seeking it.

When I discussed this with a friend she retorted: "You mean I need to go to a head shrinker?"

Her defensive remark was itself a sign of her mental and emotional condition. She needed to express her feelings and fears (she was not aware of some of them) with a trusted physician and/or psychologist. Do not consider these people head shrinkers. When your auto tires need balancing you have it done. If your thoughts or feelings are unbalanced you need to have them fixed too.

Remember we are all a little neurotic.

Symptoms get exaggerated prior to your monthly periods and during menopause. So please, if you are at all sensitive to yourself, realize the need for help when you feel everyone else is wrong.

I'm reminded of a friend who has four children spaced over ten years. She is a good mother. Her one problem has been overprotectiveness.

She has had a rough time letting loose of the three oldest. Over a span of another ten years she did manage to achieve semi-relinquishment. When the youngest child graduated from high school she was encouraged to enter a local college. I say "encouraged" because she was not pushed.

The girl was told that IF she stayed around she could have a car and all the freedom she wanted while living at home.

She stayed around. Soon she fell in love and became frustrated. The boy was nice but the mother felt he only had sex on his mind.

She did not want her daughter to get hooked with marriage or babies at the height of her education. She was not about to—but her mother and father grew so uptight about the situation that she silently threatened to run off to avoid the constant hassling.

This example, with a little variation, relates to more than a few women.

Do you fear the time when the nest will be empty? What will you do? You may even feel your life has been spent. Now there is nothing left.

When this happens, talk to a qualified person who can help you gain perspective.

Although I'm not rushing the present because I have never been happier or more blessed, I am looking forward to the middle and later years.

The period following the children's departure can be the golden years. They can be the most beautiful time of your life if you become sensitive and spiritual. The golden years are the time to do all those things you could not (or thought you could not) do earlier when you were tied down.

Mrs. Reed epitomizes this type of woman. She had two children. One died in infancy. She and her husband accepted the child's death as God's will. The other child was loved but not spoiled. They adopted another son.

After the boys were grown she visited them often —but never uninvited. After the passing of her devoted husband, Mrs. Reed developed her talents for painting and embroidery. She took courses and entered art and craft shows.

Her involvement in the church was only average, but then she discovered that there was more to life than being a grandmother and entering exhibits. She dedicated her life completely to Christ.

The last time I heard from Mrs. Reed, she was planning to be a dorm mother to the children of missionaries in the Middle East.

In a letter she said: "I will deeply miss not seeing my six grandchildren and nine great-grandchildren. However, I know where my rightful place is. I must do what God wants me to do. My own children are secure and have one another. I have a great deal of love to give, and the children that must be away from their parents need what I have."

A marvelous use of life! The love and understanding she can bring these children surely will have an impact for multiplied lifetimes.

Perhaps for eternity.

On Conflicts

All personal relationships involve certain conflicts. You are vulnerable whenever you encounter someone.

Personality Conflicts

As an individual you possess personality traits that can clash with those of others. You are in for trouble unless you are sensitive to the possibility of collision.

To be aware of a potential problem—and know how to handle conflict—is a talent.

Conflict between you and your lover is likely to crop up if you are more highly educated, passionate, clever, or stronger physically than he. Conflict between you and your lover, apartment mates, or children may arise if you are overly neat and they tend to clutter, or if you can ignore a clutter while they want everything spotless.

If you are single, carefully weigh imbalances before you have a love affair or choose new roommates. If you are married and personality conflict is a problem, use discretion. You have the perfect climate to practice your growing sensitivity. Zero in on your problem. When do you notice conflict with your husband? When he is tired? When you are? On weekends? Never on Friday? Why is it when it is? What does conflict seem to involve? Money? Children? Housekeeping? Can you recognize where you are overbearing and cause a conflict (you may have been unaware of it)? Are you being reasonable? Could you do something to sidestep the conflict before it arises? You are making headway. To understand a conflict is to be able to find a solution.

Take the case of imbalance between abilities of husband and wife. A husband is not threatened by a wife who is superior or dominant in certain areas when he sees and knows he has his own particular strong points. Praise your man for his strong points. Sincerely and naturally of course, no one likes a fake. Show him how much his talents mean to you.

Financial Conflict

Frequently the most formidable conflict a marriage encounters is finances. Each of us has been raised with certain concepts of how to save, spend, or squander money. One of the first things a couple must determine is who will manage the money—

and how.

Early in our marriage my husband and I decided to share equal responsibility for our finances. We have taken turns balancing the checkbook and itemizing the budget. No matter who is handling the books we both know where the money goes each month. We are a team. We are striving for the same goals.

There is no need for finances to be a problem if you have established communication and consideration. Turning money management over to a wife can be a hurdle that is hard for some men to clear. Unless such a husband understands that the wife is on his team, also being frugal, he will only hand out enough money for food and household maintenance.

Your man is probably the primary breadwinner. You may supplement the income (in rare cases your income may even exceed his) but he is, by Scriptural authority, the head of the house—a house that could never become a home without you.

Most conflict will arise chiefly when you put yourself in competition with your husband. Recognize the spheres where he is king, and chances are he will see you as queen in those where you excel. Together, as partners, you can make a royal pair.

I'm so Tired

Fatigue is a household word. Too many women think they are falling apart when all they need is a change of pace. Your lover should be aware of this (he will if he joins you in becoming sensitive).

Why do you think you feel so tired all the time? There could be a number of possibilities for it. You may feel a lack of fulfillment because nothing is ever finished. You begin a project. Before long the phone rings. Then you must run an errand. By the time you return it is time to fix dinner. Perhaps you should keep your projects smaller. Don't become apathetic.

You *can* control the amount of work you do in a given time.

If you are a professional woman, as well as a mother, your fatigue may stem in part from your double role. You can almost wear yourself out just by thinking about the responsibilities of both jobs. Are you sure that you should really be doing both? Are you demanding too much perfection of yourself in each role? As a current book reminds us—floors don't have to be clean enough to eat from—they aren't plates.

Talk to any gynecologist, and he will tell you that many women come to him with what they think must be some dreaded disease. Actually it is only fatigue.

What is the relationship of fatigue to sex? If you are one of those rare women who never seems to get tired, then I will tell you:

You crawl into bed, let out a little groan, and quietly say, "I'm so tired."

Your lover says, "But why?"

You try to explain, but you can't.

Soon he comes to learn that that exhausted moan means you are too tired for any activity. He may comment (after the groan and before your remark): "I know, dear, you are awfully tired."

As a lover, you are a flop. When that time comes you better do something about your "fatigue."

The working woman is likely to become incompatible with her lover because of the strain and stress of the labor world. This is generally, but by no means always, true. Men find this a problem too.

Lovemaking, nonetheless, should not always be avoided just because you are tired. Often sex can be refreshing. In fact, the National Institute of Health has stated that sexual relations are a good physical exercise!

Nervous energy also brings on fatigue. Don't let a doctor stuff you full of tranquilizers. Learn to set your own pace and to enjoy little moments of quiet.

Religious Conflict

Religion is often a point of conflict between husband and wife. If yours is an interfaith marriage, there have probably been mixed feelings within each of you. If discussion of religion proved distressing you may have even decided just not to talk about it.

Some couples end the conflict—at least outwardly—by neither one attending church. It seems a shame to force each other to voluntarily cut one's self off from spiritual fellowship. Inner turmoil may still exist, and lead to other basic conflicts. Perhaps the solution is to allow each partner to be true to his own conscience and belief and to resist the continual urge to convert. Time, and God, often have a way of resolving religious conflict. Quit fighting and put it in God's hand.

Works of the Flesh

Last, but in no way least among the conflicts marrieds face, is what the Bible calls "works of the flesh." (If you (or your husband) have been tempted and involved in any of the works of the flesh (Galatians 5:19-21; Colossians 3:5-10), you need to search yourself and seek forgiveness.)

In Colossians 3 we are warned to put away these evils: anger, wrath, malice, slander, and foul talk. We are told not to lie to one another.

I find it interesting these things are listed in the Bible. Basically we are little different now than people who lived before and during the time of Christ.

Works of the flesh become serious conflicts because they drive a wedge into a marriage relationship.

When our sexual needs are met by our husbands

41

we find we are less prone to these evils—as modern as today and as ancient as the Garden of Eden. When our bodies are relaxed and our minds secure we are less inclined to hurt a loved one.

You do have the time and the energy to create a beautiful love affair if you will use sensitivity to overcome conflicts and meet your needs and those of your lover, family, and friends.

5

ARE YOU LISTENING

Several weeks ago we were visiting some friends, and we were discussing the past weeks events. John had been on a hunting trip and Joan, his wife, had entertained her bridge club at their home. The hunting trip was exciting and John enjoyed explaining in detail about the harrowing experiences he had been through in order to get his deer. Joan, on the other hand, did not care for hunting, let alone the taste of deer meat. All she could think about was the fun she had at the bridge party. When John started telling about the fun they had in the evenings, Joan would insert little tidbits about her bridge party. Before long they were both talking at the same time. It was difficult for us to understand either of them, and John and Joan were not hearing each other.

Marriages and friendships have been ruined because of communication breakdown. When a person becomes sensitive, he becomes aware of who is talking. He hears what they are saying, and senses why it needs to be said. Faulty listening is a symptom of our society. We are losing the ability to listen creatively. It is our responsibility to know and attempt to understand what is being said by the person speaking to us, and to give him ample time to say it. Have you, for instance, experienced the frustration of having to hurry through what you were saying so as not to lose your "listener's" attention?

Learning to Listen

Here is a brief exercise for you to try. Turn on the television. Listen to any two consecutive programs other than news shows. After they are over, ask yourself: What was the main idea of each program? What did I gain from the programs? Why were the programs shown? How can I apply something of the programs to my life? This is an exercise you could also try with a friend. The answers to the above questions could be more revealing if neither of you knew what to look for ahead of time.

Chances are you may not be able to pick out a main idea in the program. You will discover the program was strictly for entertainment, and you have nothing to apply to your life style. For twenty years we have been raising children, and pacifying ourselves, with the Boob Tube. Now we wonder why people do not listen to us more attentively. We puzzle over the lack of creativity in our children. A report from The Committee on Children's Television states that the average child by age 18 has spent 11,000 hours in the classroom and 15,000 hours watching television. Children spend as much as 50 hours per week or 64 percent of their waking time watching television. By the time a child has watched a rerun it is no wonder he has learned to tune out.

The time has come for us to analyze when and why we tune out. John and Joan tuned each other out because each felt what he had to say was more important. Often we are in the presence of someone who is known for his repetitious conversations. Instead of hearing the same thing over again, we look pleasing and tune him out.

Are you listening with one ear and thinking with the other? We can listen about five times as fast as we can speak. Perhaps it would be wise to use the time lapse to analyze what the person is trying to tell us through his words, expressions, and emotions.

We are often involved in a conversation with someone when children are around or when we are in a public place. We are distracted by sights, sounds, and smells around us. We need to tune the distractions out and give all our attention to the conversation.

The sensitive woman needs to be a good listener in order to keep a conversation moving. It is important to get to know the man you are dating, or the man you married. Attempt to understand him through his facial expressions, the movements of his hands, and the tone of his voice as well as through what he is verbally expressing.

The woman between 25 and 40 was considered the now generation 10 years ago. She was never going to get old. She was always going to be relevant. Her children were going to benefit from her youthfulness.

She just knew her love life was going to be different from her parents'. Affection and endearing words were always going to be evident. She was going to be open and honest. She was going to communicate!

What happened? Her intentions were good. Is the dream still possible?

I know what happened. She became involved in social, civic, and religious groups. She married, and her husband became wrapped up in his work. Children came, and children's activities involved her time. She chose a career, and it became almost a 24-hour-a-day activity.

Perhaps this is your greatest frustration. You are not what you dreamed of being.

Do you feel that your children do not appreciate your efforts? They cry when they are hungry, walk through the house with muddy boots, can't understand why you do not take them where they want to go RIGHT NOW; and they never do anything to be helpful around the house unless you shout at them (four times)!

All this may be true. Children are like that. But do you appreciate their good qualities? Do you comment on their good marks at school (even if the teacher's only positive remark was that Johnnie "Is doing better than he used to.")?

Compliment your child on how well he dressed himself (never mind if the shirt is not perfectly tucked in, or if he got it on backwards—cheerfully help him to correct it and compliment his overall effort). Tell him or her how tall he is getting to be or how nice her hair looks.

Do not jump on a child for every little thing. Listen to his complaints—let him know you care. Treat him like you want to be treated. If you have been wrong, admit it to him. Let him see that you are trying to be a better mother as he wants to be a better child.

Children are really no different than adults when it comes to needing praise. A generation gap has been formed because too many adults feel their children are "nobodies."

What is your child trying to tell you when he throws his food on the floor, cheats in school, or starts smoking pot? You need to be a sensitive mother in order to know what he is attempting to tell you. Listen. Does the tone of his voice suggest fear, irritability, or insecurity?

Perhaps the children are not the problem. You

are confused because your marriage is not what it used to be. It just lacks something. Could it be verbal communication with your husband?

You may need to start revitalizing your approach and response—or your man may come home later and later each night. One night he may not come home at all.

Then again, he may never step out on you. He may never complain that going to bed with you has lost its zing. He may simply just ignore you as a person. (And isn't this actually emotional separation or divorce?) After all, a stereotyped, even perfunctory sexual release is easier than face-to-face encounter.

After a few years a couple feels their marriage has become "stabilized." In truth they are really quite shaky. Husband and wife both think they know all there is to know about each other. Each stops wanting to learn more about his spouse. Their lives are all enmeshed with work and children.

No wonder so many marriages break up. The husband shuts up the wife by hiding behind his newspaper. He peers out from behind it long enough to bellow some unkind words. This sends the wife storming to another room to brood and build up more defenses.

A doctor-psychologist has said that 80 percent of all marriages today are held together only because of children, or because of fear of what the church or neighbors might think if the marriage breaks up. Are you in that 80 percent?

Tom and Jane were married twenty years ago. They had four children and enjoyed many good times together. By the time the oldest daughter went off to college, Tom was firmly established in a business of his own. They moved to another community to be closer to his work.

Instead of growing closer together during this time after the children were gone, they became more distant. Dialogue had broken down, and each was going his own way. He was away on business much of the time. She got a job and patiently waited for him to come home.

This happens too frequently. Couples forget to look back at why they married. The glow of loving partnership fades.

Several years ago the couples' group in our church spent several evenings discussing the need to keep marriage vibrant.

The project culminated with a re-marriage service in the sanctuary. Each couple pretended they were alone. The pastor read the marriage vows, and the couples repeated the "I do's" to each other.

I have never seen so much love transferred through glances!

After the ceremony the couples attended a reception and had the opportunity to talk about the experience. Every couple (there were twelve) felt their marriage had had a shot in the arm. All are still married.

If engaged couples could look on their coming marriage not as a love that will last, but as a love that will grow, they would have a foundation that would not crumble.

Sometimes couples need to sit down together to a candlelight dinner for two.

It's fun to laugh about the days of your youth; to recall certain dates that brought joy and happiness.

When was the last time you thought about the excitement prior to your marriage? Or looked at your wedding pictures? When did you last remember the vows of the ceremony, or laugh over your honeymoon experiences? Can you recall the excitement of the first child?

An Exercise to Do: Plan a cozy evening for two. Ship your children off to grandmother, or swap stay-over nights with a friend who also has children. Do something your husband completely enjoys and you can share together—see a ball game, go to a concert. Make it a special night for two lovers in love.

As you begin to seriously examine your relationship with your mate, you may feel that you are beyond the limits of re-establishing loving relationships as simply as suggested above. If this is the case—if major barriers and tensions are evident—you may need to examine your problem from a new perspective. Additional steps, such as the following may have to be taken.

First: face and define the problem to the best of your ability (and if it seems clear that professional help is needed, don't hesitate to seek it). *Second:* try to determine where, when and how the problem began; then begin at that point to set things right. *Three:* prayerfully and carefully—at the right moment (which God will help you find), discuss your findings and feelings with your mate—and begin to rebuild the bridge.

As you build (or rebuild) a marriage, always plan time to be alone as a couple. This is especially necessary after children arrive.

A friend of mine relates: "My parents would go out once a month for a nice dinner, movie, or dessert; we kids were always aware that they were a pair of lovers, not just our parents."

This is an important concept. Not only for what it does to your relationship, but for your children's view of marriage as well.

The award-winning song, "For All We Know," popularized by the Carpenters, says it like it should be:

Love, look at the two of us,
Strangers in many ways,
We've got a lifetime to share,
So much to say.

And as we go from day to day,
I'll feel you close to me,
But time alone will tell.

Let's take a lifetime to say,
"I knew you well."
For only time will tell us so.
And love may grow, for all we know.

The middle years and beyond are some of life's richest. It never ceases to be important to keep lines of communication open.

If you are in the middle-age bracket and are perplexed because you and your lover have not been communicating at a deeper level, share your needs with your man. Perhaps invite him to join you in becoming more sensitive. It is a thrill to discover new awarenesses together. So at least look for experiences you can share that sharpen your sensitivities.

Take a good hard look at your home. What is its SQ (Sensitivity Quotient)? Is your house a hut or a home? Do you maintain it for your family with no strings attached?

An Exercise to Do: As you look thoughtfully around your house, how many little things can you see that you intend to do? Rehang some pictures? Recover a chair? Put on some paint? Get a new rug? Refinish a table? Replace some plants?

Put all these little tasks you never make time for onto a list.

Choose one project, and tackle it today, then keep after the others until you can toss away the list and enjoy the satisfactions of your labors.

Ruth Graham, wife of the famed evangelist, is a sterling example of a good homemaker. Billy is a world traveler, almost continually on the go. While she sometimes accompanies him, Mrs. Graham maintains her steady belief that the woman's place is in the home—that this is her castle.

If you are unable to feel comfortably at home in the house for which you are responsible, then get some help from friends or a decorating book. Use your creativity and imagination to make your home pleasant and interesting.

Think of your house as something more than a place for family members to eat and sleep. It should be filled with warmth and understanding.

Home should be a place where you are accepted for what you are. It is a place friends can come for fellowship. A place where joys and sorrows can be shared.

If you have love and sensitivity those who enter your home will be warmed—whether or not you have a fire in the fireplace.

6

SENSITIVITY AND YOUR SEXUALITY

Finally! We are ready to talk about the relationship of sensitivity to sex.

A man does not usually have any problem initiating intercourse. A woman can go through the physical act of sex fairly easly. But what does the mere mechanical act accomplish by itself?

Nothing (except possible pregnancy and physical relief)!

The union between a man and a woman is meant to be far more than mechanical manipulations. It should be both meaningful and beautiful. It should be a union of body, mind, and spirit. God did not intend for man or woman to be the object of sexploitation by the other.

In order for sex to become more than an act, a couple needs to be aware of sensations. The sensation of anticipation, expectation. The sensation of one body reaching out to the other. A brief—but lingering—moment for each one to bring the ultimate in sexual fulfillment. This is our goal.

To obtain this quality you must make an investment.

Since intercourse involves two people, barriers to sensitivity are almost inevitable. Some interfere with the mind, but they affect the physical response.

Barriers include environment, hygiene, attire, and the lack of understanding and openness a couple may face within their marriage.

You may discover others.

Let's begin with the environment. Look at your home. The place your lover will enter after a hard day at work. (Maybe it wasn't a hard day, but he is coming home to *you*, isn't he?)

What is the first thing that hits him when he walks in the door? Is there an atmosphere of calmness? A feeling of comfort? Perhaps the fresh aroma and beauty of a simple flower arrangement or a favorite dish.

Clutter inhibits relaxation for some people. If you do nothing else during the day, pick up that living room! Have a place ready for a cup of tea or a glass of something cool to drink for your man when he gets home.

Chances are his day has been scheduled for him. He has been on the go. Now you are greeting him with serenity and a place where he can relax and unwind.

Two other rooms must be kept clean: the bathroom and the bedroom.

Rest rooms at work are cold, barren, tile places. He probably has been using paper towels, hot-air blowers, or semi-grimy cloth towels that roll around and around to dry his hands and face.

Clean jacquard towels, a throw rug on the floor, a small vase of flowers, and crisp curtains on your bathroom windows will go over with the man in your life. These little touches affect a softness that speaks of you and makes a house a home.

You spend a third of your life together in the bedroom (at least you should). You are not awake all that time, but the mood you set when you are may determine the quality of rest you get.

A friend used to complain to me how she desired her husband to make love to her. By the time he picked up the vacuum from the middle of the floor, put away his clothes, and took the children's toys to their respective rooms, he was ready for sleep!

He felt his wife should do those chores during the day (she should have), and he resented having to do them. He punished his spouse by depriving her of sexual relations.

Women play that little game with their husbands too. But is that what love is all about? Do your best to keep the house the way you think your husband likes it. He will usually hurry home if you do.

Last—but not least—use candles or oil lamps for a cozy atmosphere. I give candles as bridal-shower gifts, and with them I tell about the beauty of love by candlelight.

While your man is showering—get yours before he does—turn down the bed, place a little perfume behind your ear (more on this later), and light the candles. Then snap off the lights!

A final word: All this preparation will be wasted if you use candles that drip. Nothing thwarts love-making like the smell of melted wax burning a dresser top. Use dripless candles or the kind in little glass containers.

* * *

An Exercise to Do: Call a friend to join you, and visit your nearest candle shop. Allow yourself time to browse noting the colors, shapes, and scents of the various candles.

Choose one special candle that will blend harmoniously with your bedroom, and treat yourself to it.

* * *

Not only should the atmosphere surrounding

your husband be pleasing; the sight directly before him should delight his eyes. You!

I know what it is like to have children and to keep up with daily tasks. Or a job. But I try to have my face washed and my hair combed when my man comes home. Better yet, I try to have on fresh clothes. When time permits, I shower before his arrival.

P.S. FOR MEN ONLY (in case you, a male reader, find yourself reading this book). Sensitivity is for men, too. If you want to be a real man, there are some things you can do which will increase your lover's sensitivity. For instance: phone her if you are going to be late, so she won't worry. Bring flowers or something special from the bakery that she loves. Bring her a little gift on occasion.

Freshen up before dinner. Keep yourself presentable, neat and pleasant. Important: treat your lady like you did on one of your first dates. Do all of this gradually (or the shock may be too much for her). But don't fall back to your old routine. Whatever you do, remember, there is no substitute for you—giving yourself (not material things only) to your mate!

Our men are vulnerable. They may see many young women during the day who are dressed as if they just walked out of the latest fashion magazine. Don't let it throw you if your man looks at these women, but make sure that when he arrives home he also has something equally nice to look at that is his alone.

Better still, your squeezable, warm, and receptive body may be the only thing that will erase some of the scars of the day.

Once a week every woman should have an hour or so in the bathroom—uninterrupted—to groom her body. I believe in the "natural" look. I also believe in a manicured (groomed) look.

* * *

After a few years of marriage and several children, many women find they have neglected their figures or their wardrobe. (Neglect of one usually leads to carelessness for the other.)

Styles are varied and most anything goes these days. A few things, however, are really "in". Try to have at least one outfit that wows your husband. Dress in his favorite colors. I'm not saying conform to him completely, but do take him into consideration. After all, aren't you dressing to please him?

One of the most exciting things to me is to have my husband go with me to buy a dress. He delights to have me try on all the outfits that he has chosen. He hates shopping—but when it comes to getting me something he has admired or has in mind—it is a different story.

Maintain your present wardrobe and bring it up to date as you add bit by bit.

Give special thought to your evening attire. There are nights when you need a warm gown or pajamas, but select a pair that opens down the front and has some frills or bows. At least look feminine—not like a football player or a witch.

Give the novelty sleepwear a try. Keep your man guessing what's coming off next.

Speaking about taking it off . . . it might be a good idea to give some thought to your figure. Equip your bathroom with a reliable scale so you can watch what happens to you weight-wise.

You can always find magazines that have crash programs to get in shape. Diets, exercises, and yoga are in vogue. Health spas are springing up across the country. They promise a hefty weight loss and a new you within a month.

I've tried all the trimming techniques. When it

comes right down to it, getting in shape is up to you. Only you can decide whether you will be a maxi-body in a mini-suit on the beach.

Watch your carbohydrates, sweets, and between-meal snacks and the problem will be half-licked. To lick the other half, exercise by walking, jogging, or doing simple exercises regularly. The Air Force physical fitness program is good, and it outlines a routine for gradually building up exercise.

An Exercise to Do: Find your daughter's jumping rope, or make a note to buy yourself one the next time you shop.

Set a time in your daily schedule—while the bacon cooks, just before lunch, whenever it is convenient for you to give yourself five minutes. Jump the rope as long as you can each day until you build your time up to five minutes, then jump regularly every day.

* * *

You will get discouraged about your diet. You will find it difficult to exercise. Before you quit, think about those nights by candlelight when your body is given to your husband.

Psychologically, a curvaceous figure can do wonders for your eagerness and ability for love play. The well-proportioned body is beautiful. It was made for love. If a velvet ribbon around your neck is all you want to wear at bedtime—great!

But watch out. There probably won't be much talk about the day. . . .

* * *

Before the time you seriously considered getting married you read and talked about sex. You may have picked up some misinformation along the way. Possibly you expected ecstacy on your wedding night, and you may have been (or will be) disappointed.

Young woman, enjoy the love within you on that

57

night! Don't expect perfection. Your man must know this too. Frustration is frequent—but normal. Lack of sensitivity is the biggest handicap; inexperience is another.

Tell your man how much love play you need, what you like and dislike. Likewise, be sensitive to his need for caressing—and know when to go easy. You who have been or are married know how important this is.

Don't hesitate to talk about your needs. It is senseless to suffer in silence. Foreplay and intercourse are more enjoyable and are a deeper expression of love when there is openness and sensitivity.

Some women are super-sexed; others could not care less. These are extremes. The important thing is how you can please your lover. Whatever you and your partner do is acceptable as long as neither of you finds doing it unpleasant or objectionable.

Know how to turn on your lover, but be discreet. Some days all you want is lovemaking; other times you want to cool it. That is where communication comes in. How is your husband and lover going to know your highs, lows, and in-betweens unless you tell him how you feel?

Until I opened lines of communication with my husband he had to guess my moods (by my actions). Some were not so pleasing, he told me later in gentle understatement.

I know women who never outgrew that stage. Their husbands have gone looking for communication elsewhere.

Glandular problems also hinder sexual adjustment. We tend to forget that intercourse is a normal bodily function.

If too much time elapses between sex acts, a

man's semen accumulates and it may make it more difficult for him to delay his ejaculation. Thus there may not be enough time for the woman to reach orgasm.

The problem of premature ejaculation may be overcome if you are attentive to your man's needs. Don't become too busy with trivialities at bedtime. He needs you!

Men, usually more easily aroused visually than women, have a tendency to look at curvaceous bodies. If your man's sexual appetite is satisfied at home, he will be able to admire—but not lust after —attractive women he sees or meets. He will come to you for intimate relations.

Another factor that influences sexual relations is the menstrual cycle. Because of a chemical imbalance over the twenty-eight days (more or less) of your cycle, your sexual desire will vary. Nature's plan is to make you most interested in relations on the tenth to twelfth days after your period.

That is not to say you will not have desires at other times. You probably will. Ninety percent of men can be instantly aroused while only thirty percent of women have this capability. Should you have intercourse during your period? If you and your lover do not mind there is not any reason why you should not make love.

Keep your man in mind. His desires do not fluctuate as much as yours. He is likely to be raring to go most any night. You will receive enjoyment through meeting his needs.

Sexual inhibitions cause some of the greatest hang-ups encountered by those age 25 and over. Puritanical attitudes in the home often produce these emotional and psychological frustrations. If parents would only realize how prudishness and ignorance harms their children.

The girl's mother is usually responsible for passing on false views, such as old wives' tales. One non sequitur: "Painful monthly periods mean intercourse will be painful."

Inhibitions are occasionally caused by unattractive physical features, such as obesity, scars, and birthmarks. These can often be corrected or minimized through diets, cosmetics, and surgery.

If you are inhibited by physical problems, you should make every effort to overcome them. Think of yourself as having something (sensitivity) to give to someone else.

Two other fears—opposite sides of the same coin—often inhibit sex. They are fear of pregnancy and fear of infertility.

If you fear getting pregnant because of inadequate finances, the need to finish educational plans, or because you think pregnancy or delivery might be painful, talk with your gynecologist and he will advise you.

Contraceptives and other means of family planning are safe and usually reliable. Commonly used contraceptives include the Pill and intrauterine devices (IUD). Other types are the diaphragm, foams and jellies, and condoms (used by the man).

Not long ago a woman with five nearly grown children told me she thought part of the problem of her sex life was that her husband did not want any more children. I asked her what method of birth control she used.

Her reply: "None."

No wonder relations were strained! I told her to see her gynecologist—pronto.

Other women fear infertility. The bliss of birth control can become a spreading groundless dread that it is not the contraceptives that are keeping you from getting pregnant. You cannot conceive!

This fear is often transmitted to a young girl through her mother. She often says something like this to her daughter: "I imagine you will have trouble conceiving. I had such a difficult time. It is hereditary, you know."

No, it is not!

If you were told this tale, forget it.

Sometimes a young woman will think unceasingly about what she will do if she cannot get pregnant. She works out adoptions in her mind. She thinks about artificial insemination. Unfortunately she is so wrapped up in her thoughts that she ties her body in knots and brings upon herself the very thing she dreads—infertility.

Emotional hang-ups are not the only cause of infertility, but they are something to be considered. One out of ten marriages is infertile. About half of these marriages can be helped to eventually produce a child.

Months and years of infertility can be emotionally wearing on a couple. It takes maturity on the part of both to go through doctor visits, counseling, and —on occasion—make love for lab tests.

If you have an infertility problem, talk to a doctor. Realize that fears may be groundless; if you are intellectually informed and physically healthy, it will help you solve your problem. If there should be a physical impediment, worry will only aggravate it anyway.

If inhibitions are your hangup, answer the following questions. Think through your answers:

1. What was I taught about sex?

2. How many of these teachings are fact? Fancy? (If you're not sure, ask your doctor.)

3. Do I avoid love play because I do not want to be touched? Or because I dislike the act of intercourse itself?

4. Could I give in to what my husband would enjoy without it being greatly unpleasant to me?

If you are embarrassed to have your husband touch you—that is an inhibition. You can deal with this intellectually by using the above questions. You can deal with the problem practically by heeding what is said in this book about the joys of love play.

Many couples have beautiful sex lives. Still, fatigue, sickness, and temporary strains may make either the man or the woman unable to reach orgasm. Show tenderness when this happens to your mate. Don't let frustration, irritability, or resentment stifle future love play.

Men have related problems too. A man who is afraid of impotency can cause heartache for his lover as well as himself.

You can help by your sympathy, love, and positive remarks. Never ridicule or show irritation.

Janice's husband had been on duty for a year in Viet Nam. She expected a passionate session when he got back. Surprise! He headed straight for bed—and sleep.

She let him.

It had been a difficult year of separation. Instead of quizzing him about a possible affair overseas or what was wrong with him, she expressed her joy at his being home. Then she curled up beside him and dropped off to sleep too.

In time Janice learned that he feared impotency and therefore was afraid to make any overtures to her. He did not want to be a failure.

Her love, support, and patience not only helped her husband overcome his problem, but it also brought a deeper dimension of understanding to their marriage.

The problem of infection can also throw a monkey wrench into sexual adjustment. Various vaginal disorders seem to occur for no reason. This is just part of being a woman.

Use proper hygiene after intercourse. At the first sign of vaginal infection see your doctor. With proper treatment, your sex life should not suffer—unless your husband develops the same problem. If that is the case, you have double trouble. You should both see your doctor, and be patient!

Most barriers to a satisfactory sex life can be overcome by common sense, sensitivity, intellectual understanding, and experience. The barricades can be swept away—if you are willing to work at it.

7

SENSITIVITY TO
THE MAN IN YOUR LIFE

Hopefully by now you are coming to know yourself better through your senses; you are aware of needs and conflicts. You should begin to recognize the barriers to fulfillment in your sex life.

Do you know your lover's hang-ups? What barriers does the man in your life face? How well do you know what he is feeling?

You are attracted to this man . . . in love with him. How and why do you entrance him?

His emotions, unlike yours, are less likely to run close to the surface. Underneath, though, they are every bit as strong.

Unlike you, he is far more likely to be quickly stimulated sexually. The way you look at him, talk to him, touch his hand can set him on fire—or turn him to ice. At the crook of your finger you can send him into orbit—or in search of someone who will.

You need to understand this male creature, his physiology, what makes him turn on, what turns him off.

An Exercise to Do: How long has it been since you read a good reference on male physiology? If your answer is longer than six months, you can probably use a refresher. Plan a visit to your local library or bookstore where you can obtain a reliable commentary about how a man functions.

As you read, think of ways to apply the information you glean toward building a better sexual communication.

Your man's self-image is at least a partial reflection of how you look at him. Unless he married you because he needed a mother figure, he wants to feel he is in charge—that you view him as one who will care for and protect you.

Women's Lib is hurting our men because it attempts to deny them what is rightfully theirs. I'm not saying women do not have a place in the professional world, or that they do not deserve equal rights and pay—they do. But women are stripping men of their protective rights: those nice little things a man can do to show he cares.

What man feels in charge when he takes his wife out for the evening and she jumps out of the car before the ignition is turned off? What husband and father feels like the man of the house when he is only a "yes" man dominated by a matriarchy?

Yet there are times when a man likes to revert to a pampered role.

You can easily understand how he feels when he is sick. This is a time when he needs babying: his meals in bed, a back rub, a favorite dish, a cup of tea with the evening paper.

Don't tell him I said so, but it is because of this attention that he does not mind being sick; all this makes him feel cared for and loved.

But what about you?

One of women's greatest complaints about their husbands is that they just don't seem to care.

Early in his marriage, the husband is beginning to get established in a career. There are demands on him from his boss or men in the office. Until he married you he was a tiger on the loose. Now he has a tigress to care for!

If he is a man who loves his social life, and if you are working as well as keeping house, then you may see him frustrated when you insist on a good night of rest.

When the little tiger cubs come along, he begins to feel the financial pinch.

He may think all his labors are going down the drain. At times he is elated, and at times he is depressed. These moods may be directly tied to ups and downs in his job or profession.

You need sensitivity to understand his fears, frustrations, and fancies. You need to help him gain perspective. Your sensitivity will pay off if you are able to detect his needs—especially at the end of the day.

When your man is around 40-50 he is likely to steer off course—usually temporarily. About that time he is responsible for the weddings of daughters and the education of sons. This is the time he is probably making more money than ever before—and maybe more than he will in the future.

If he only has eyes for his work—and not for you —again you need that sensitivity we are talking about.

When you are in one of those *neurotic* moods (and I use that word purposely because that is exactly the way we are when we are not mentally and emotionally balanced), you may have sometimes thought about what a soft life your husband has.

After all, he has a plush office with thick carpeting and mahogany paneling. Or at least he works in an air-conditioned building, while you sweat over mounds of ironing in a steamy kitchen.

He does not have to worry about jostling kids for an hour or so in a noisy reception room waiting to see the doctor or the dentist.

He does not have to feed the peanut-butter and jelly sandwich to the baby or clean up the spilled milk.

Instead, he can go out with the men, sit down to a well-appointed table, and savor a gourmet luncheon.

Yet where would you be without his job? What about the chic outfit he gave you? Or the vacation you are planning together at that romantic hideaway?

Here again we lack sensitivity if we clobber our man with petty jealousies or the self-pity bit.

*   *   *

Your man's sexual desire is subject to variation depending on his health, energy, and things on his mind.

A man's mind is flexible, yet it is the strongest controlling mechanism he possesses.

He is capable of sexual fantasies, of daydreaming, of creating vast financial empires, and of abject feelings of defeat.

A mental picture of an attractive undraped female can so stir his imagination that he is ready for instant sex.

It is obvious you need to understand what goes on in his mind. The only way to be at the center of his thoughts is to yield yourself to him. Be so fascinating that he will not be tempted to let his thoughts wander for long.

A man is eager to share his inner feelings with a devoted wife. A man is more than enthusiastic to come home to a sexy wife. You hold the key to his self-concept. You can make or break him. In doing so, you can build or break your marriage.

Your lover needs a "three-in-one" woman: *sincere, sensitive,* and *sensuous.*

Too many women use love as a way to get something they want. Others connive in order to keep their husbands in the dark about their activities or their money-spending.

A man has to have faith in his wife. He must trust her. Once that trust is broken by insincerity, he begins to wonder when he can believe her.

If you have a tendency to be a little less than candid about what you tell your man, better begin to be totally honest.

Not long ago I complimented a friend on a new outfit she had made. She confided that the material was not on sale as she had told her husband. But she just *had* to have it, she explained.

Her husband, not knowing the latest prices in fabrics, never knew the difference. She told him it was on sale to make him think it had been a bargain. He will never know—unless he walks by the yardage one day and finds the price the same as his wife paid.

Every wife (and every couple) should have one of the following books beside her bed for further reading (there are many more that can helpfully pull the marriage together): *Sexual Happiness in Marriage,* Herbert J. Miles, Zondervan, Grand Rapids, Michigan (paper .95), and *The Marriage Affair,* J. Allan Peterson, Tyndale House, Wheaton, Illinois (paper, 420 pages, $2.95).

An Exercise to Do: Before bedtime tonight, sit down and read a tender love story out of one of your favorite magazines or collections of short stories. Relax as you read, and let yourself drift along with the mood of the story. You will be surprised what it does to prepare for bed.

A man is like a child who wants a new toy.

A man would like to find new adventure with his wife, and if he can't . . . he may be sorely tempted to seek it elsewhere.

Perhaps it is a difficult thing for you to cooperate with your husband's desires for experimentations—new positions, new technique. Your background may have been such that you learned it somehow was not right to try what your husband suggests. It is wrong only out of the bonds of marriage. Within marriage nearly anything goes if it is mutual and wholesome.

When a husband and wife love each other they have an urge to share it. This means to do what feels good. Attempt to let loose.

Signals from a man's brain are sent to the various parts of his body. And vice versa. A woman associates the penis and scrotum as the center of a man's sexual life. These are the primary areas, just as the clitoris and the vagina are the principal parts of a woman's body from which she derives sexual pleasure.

It must be remembered, however, that sexual stimulation also comes through such parts of the body as the ears, neck, abdominal region, and—one of the most important of all—the lips.

Almost nothing stimulates your man more than placing your relaxed lips on his. Allow the warmth of your love to be transmitted as your relaxed body melts into his.

A tense kiss, a rigid body, or a light squeeze are about as exciting to your man as a clinch with a mannequin.

Speaking of new adventure and experimentation, here is a *Passion Pack* guaranteed to turn on your lover. Some of the suggestions may seem way out. Before you pass judgment, give it a try. See if your man doesn't find you more sensuous.

1 very sheer nightgown (for candlelight evenings).
1 bikini-type novelty bra and briefs (to catch your man off guard).
1 velvet ribbon—his favorite color (add more colors gradually); fasten around the neck with a small pin (to be worn when he has been preoccupied).
1 bottle of his favorite perfume (caution: may be habit forming).
1 candle (to fill the room with the glow of romance).

At times a man just is not able to function sexually. This is not too often—but it can happen. You should be aware of these times.

The middle years are the time most men fear impotency—the inability to perform intercourse and ejaculate—but, impotency may occur any time. Most men experience temporary impotency sometime during life but this is nothing alarming.

If a woman harasses her husband and wants to know why he is not performing, she could lead him into permanent impotency.

At the beginning of this chapter I spoke about the power of the mind. This is an example of the mind often having control over the flesh. A man must believe in himself. His wife must be patient and understanding.

Erik, at 43, discovered he was unable to have an erection. He had a beautiful wife who was sexy, sensuous, and sensitive. What more could he want?

Erection is not something you make happen, but something you let happen.

When his wife realized the problem she whispered softly into Erik's ear. She expressed her love.

She told him she wanted to be close to his strong, masculine body. Her support and reassurance helped Erik regain his self-confidence.

Being downgraded or belittled can also drive a man to impotency—or to another woman.

Jessie, an outdoor woman, is athletically inclined. Her nature is competitive; she wants to be the best in everything she does.

Her husband, John, did not always do things the way she thought he should. When this happened Jessie exclaimed, "Be a man!"

When this procedure invaded the bedroom, poor John gradually performed like a eunuch rather than a man.

Belittling and nagging can literally drive a man out of the house. In the wise words of Proverbs (25:24), "It is better to dwell in the corner of the housetop, than with a brawling woman in a wide house."

Too often I've heard a wife say: "You mean you're going to watch *another* ball game? Why don't you ever get the garage cleaned out!"

Another classic nag in some marriages is: "You eat too much; you work too much." Maybe he does; nagging or criticizing will likely only aggravate matters.

* * *

There has been a recent upsurge of literature on the male menopause. Some deny it exists. Others build a convincing case for it.

Look around. Men from 40 to 65 are as apt to be going through this stage as their women counterparts.

The male menopause is not considered hormonal like women's. Male menopause is psychological. It is physiological if impotence occurs.

The man going through male menopause is plagued with indecision, restlessness, boredom, a feeling of being trapped. He often says, "What's the use?" He realizes all of a sudden that there are more years behind than years ahead.

A friend recently remarked: "I can't believe it. All of a sudden time is running out. Where have the years gone? I find myself seeking answers, but I can't come up with anything concrete. I don't know what to do."

He wants success. He wants security. He wants life.

As he thinks about it, he realizes he does not have as much money in the bank as he would like. He sees the young buck running around with sexy young girls.

He may view his wife as stable and loving, but there is nothing new. After reading the sex manuals he wants to try out some of the new techniques.

No sooner does he get excited about this than he realizes his wife would never do "that." He doesn't know how to bring up the topic with her.

Tom, a 46 year-old insurance salesman, has developed a beer belly, a receding hairline, and an insatiable desire for sex. He hears his buddies talk about their experiences with women. He feels something is lacking in his sex life.

Would an affair with another woman make him feel better?

No, he loves his wife. But he can't get enough sex.

He tries to satisfy his obsession for sex by attending X-rated movies. He reads books dealing with wild love affairs. He flirts whenever he can.

He may even try a visit to a massage parlor with all girl masseuses.

Getting together with other couples gives him an excuse to embrace the wives and occasionally kiss them upon arrival.

Tom is typical of many men in this stage of life.

So is Frank. One day he told my husband:

"I love my wife. She is good and kind; fixes great meals and does a good job at keeping house. But you know, she is so busy and so tired we never have much time for sex. When we do, I know she enjoys it because of the little sounds she makes; and so do I; but you know, it doesn't have any zing.

"Now for the good part . . . last Thursday a friend of mine said he was having a few of the boys over and to come along. I did. Do you know what I found? Some of the sexiest, curviest little chicks you ever laid eyes on.

"They weren't there to serve drinks either.

"They paired off with each of the fellows and wow! I never thought sex recreation could be so great!"

That was Frank's story. To him the variety added a zing. He had no moral or spiritual values to keep him faithful, but neither do a lot of men.

Frank, who is in his mid-forties, was made aware of the male menopause and how it can change attitudes. With this understanding he realized he had been unfaithful to his wife and their marraige vows.

He told her about his indiscretion. I had shared an early outline of this book with her, and she was beginning to be more sensitive.

Her response was, "I understand why you were tempted. You were wrong to do it, but I would be wrong not to forgive you. You have hurt me, but I love you. I need you.

"I haven't been as sexually creative as you might like. I think we should share our feelings more with each other."

Frank's wife, a fine Christian, responded maturely to a serious threat to her marriage. Others might have been inclined to say: "I'll get even with him!"

The unfortunate thing about the male menopause

is that it comes about the same time when a woman is going through her change. During the years a couple is going through this experience they should stay in contact with a physician.

Hormone shots are available for the woman. On occasion testosterone is recommended for the man if he has potency problems.

The best medicine for a man and a woman is the love and affection only they can give each other.

8

THE SEXUAL REVOLUTION

The Sexual Revolution is upon us. It confronts men and women with varying sets of values. Some young people are running to the nudie beaches while some parents are keeping their dates with the swap club. If that is not enough, the revolution boasts of Gay liberation to boot.

Part of the revolution is good; the rest is dangerous.

If you are single, you are probably seeking greater independence and possibly looking for Mr. It.

Louise came from a closely knit home in a middle class community. Her parents had protected her and given her all the basic things she needed—and a little more.

Her dream throughout high school was to go to New York where life would be exciting—not such a drag. Within weeks of her graduation she went to the city and took a job as a cleaning girl and babysitter.

Louise took care of the children and did whatever the lady of the house demanded. After a while, Louise's boss and his wife separated and got a divorce. Louise stayed on to tend the children. The oldest one was only a couple of years younger than she was.

Time passed, and Louise married her boss. Because of a ready-made family, Louise suddenly was plunged into all the responsibilities of a seasoned mother—at the tender age of 18.

The adventure of discovering a creative sex life together with her new husband was hindered because of responsibilities and the demands on Louise's time. She was so busy trying to be a mother she did not have time to be a bride.

Jennifer, a city girl was tired of her humdrum life and wanted to get out on her own. She rented an apartment in the suburbs and took a job as a computer analyst. The work was interesting and she discovered great dating possibilities.

Soon Jennifer began dating a yummy young man from her office. He told her he was divorced. They talked about their future together and how much life could mean if they were married. Jennifer took this to mean marriage was imminent. Because their love was so wonderful, she did not feel it would hurt to go to bed with him. They would be getting married soon—she thought.

An emergency brought the wife of Jennifer's lover to the office one day, and Jennifer quickly found out who she was.

The air came hissing out of her balloon in a hurry. Jennifer was flattened! What would she do with the scrapbook and the wedding plans?

Jennifer should have been more skeptical and less gullible. Perhaps she needed to play sleuth a little harder. She needed to be honest and open with her dates, and she needed to require the same of those she dated.

Many men feel no need to get deeply involved if they can find an attractive woman to bed down. If you are serious about finding a man who will be sensitive to your needs—and be around in twenty years or so—maintain your high standards. A fellow who has the same values will love you for it some day.

When love is present, passion can be subdued until the right time.

Wise singles may desire marriage—but not at any cost.

A young schoolteacher—27 and very attractive—shared with me her requirements for a husband. She felt it was better to teach and stay single than to marry one of the men she liked but did not love.

Her patience and ideals paid off. She married a man who meets her requirements and whom she loves. She is glad to have been a single woman and to have had the experiences only single people can have.

She has gained her independence and proved herself. Now her dating and debating days are over.

There are some single women who date men that never show any sexual desires. Either the man has a low need for physical expression, or there is a chance he is a homosexual.

If you suspect the latter, better do some research on this type of person. If a relationship is allowed to go too far, emotional damage could be done to both of you. (Even if you were to discover the worst at this point, you would find your emotions mixed.) In order to flee an unhappy, intense love affair Kay moved to another university. Before long she started dating a graduate student in political philosophy. A recent letter from Kay says:

"From the semester break until the day when he took me to his dormitory room, our relationship was good, but for some reason I sensed something was wrong about Doug. I couldn't put my finger on it, but it created increasing distress within me—his excessive talk about his mother and never a mention of his father. Little things.

"When I went to his room, he turned up the radio to cover the sound of his voice and said, 'Kay, I have something to tell you. I am a homosexual.'

"I went back to my dorm and had a good case of hysterics, then I wrote a kind and compassionate letter to Doug. Despite my own shock, I felt no hostility towards him; I felt only pity. He did not choose things to be this way, and he would suffer all his life."

Doug was honest. He gave Kay the power to destroy his life. He wanted to hide his homosexual characteristics but he couldn't.

Kay was wise not to try to cure Doug by herself. If you run into a similar case, seek professional help.

Your sex drive can sometimes produce major frustrations. It does not matter if you are married, divorced, widowed, or unmarried. There is nothing wrong with those yearnings and urges. They are natural. Their intensity will vary and how you handle them will be up to you. Lest you think I'm all for free love, there is more than one way to conquer the problem of sexual frustration.

One way is to divert your interest in other areas. A well-balanced single needs activities, for they contribute to mental and emotional health. It is important not to get in a rut. Many young women claim that to get in a rut is easy to do—especially when you are new to an area and have not established yourself.

In many cities there are YWCAs and college and career groups in churches and synagogues. Ask about their programs. Some cities have ski clubs and a variety of other organizations that promote social gatherings and sports events.

There are times when a well-adjusted couple will hit the sexual doldrums. They may begin reading literature on spouse swapping. Maybe another couple will share experiences with them and invite them to a get-together.

Spouse swapping, as well as several other couple games, is on the increase. These encounters all involve nudity and probably sexual relations with a different partner or partners. Some are multiple affairs—better known as orgies.

The scene of these swap clubs is often a sophisticated suburban home. The couples are usually screened by the couple originating the club.

To the outsider it might seem like just another party—at first. They would find drinks, laughter, music, dancing, and chit-chat. After awhile someone might show a pornographic movie. Guests might begin stripping or doing suggestive dances.

After an hour or so of preliminaries the men pair off with women—not their wives—and disappear to another room, or home. In some cases the men might swap keys. Each man would go home with the woman whose house key he had drawn.

Some swap groups meet as often as three to four times a week. If a marriage needs sexual expression, and if a couple is with other partners three to four times a week, this does not leave much extra time—unless sex is one's only outside interest!

Couples who belong to swap clubs are always looking for good prospects. Most claim swapping adds excitement—and gusto—to a marriage.

Don't you believe it!

Swappers have copped out.

If you put the same effort into your personal sexual relationships with your husband as you would put into preparing for and attending a swap party you will have a secure, sensuous sex life of your own. Your very own.

Proponents of the swap claim it has a stabilizing influence in a marriage. *The theory:* frequent practice with many sexual partners improves sex within the marriage bonds. The relationship between the swappers is safe because no love is involved. No attachments are to be formed.

I wonder how you can have the intimate sexual contact with another person and not run the risk of some attachment—even if it is an unhealthy one. Sex without love does little to stabilize a marriage. It simply becomes a commodity to be traded.

Swappers prefer to call their parties sex laboratories rather than orgies. Swappers are free from the fear of pregnancy because the code requires strict contraceptive measures, usually taken by the men.

Club members claim there are no guilt feelings about these extra-curricular relations because your partner is there doing the same thing you are. It is not infidelity, they say, because it is done with mutual knowledge and consent. In another setting the same activity would be called "cheating" and could therefore become grounds for divorce.

Think about those beautiful moments of passion you and your husband have shared. Can you visualize him in bed with someone else—perhaps even a friend—attempting to have the same ecstatic moment?

Multiple-mating is still considered illegal. William R. Breedlove in "Swap Clubs and the Law," (*The Magazine of Modern Sex*, Vol. 1, No. 2 September, 1964, page 124—used by permission)—observes:

"Every state in the Union has laws that dictate when and how two individuals may not copulate, even though that copulation may be in private and by mutual consent."

Not only are people being sinful when they participate in this sport, they are violating the law as well.

Swap proponents argue that our society must abolish codes concerning the practice of private sexual behavior. They say we must see ourselves as part of the "developing post-Judeo-Christian trend in sex and morals."

I can't accept that and I won't. I have seen too many men and women develop beautiful love affairs because of their relationship to God through Christ.

Authorities claim that five to eight million men and women in the United States have experimented with mate switching. Some of your friends may be among them.

One day while discussing this part of the book with a friend, I discovered there was a swap group in my own neighborhood. Several weeks beforehand I would have been shocked. Not now. This sort of promiscuity goes on everywhere.

We must speak out against it.

If your sex life is shabby, don't use that as an excuse to commit adultery. Develop some of your own techniques to add zest to your marriage.

Join the Sexual Revolution by forming your own club. Limit the membership to two.

Several women have spoken to me about masturbation. Is it right or wrong? People used to think it was harmful to the sex organs and could even cause senility.

That is simply untrue. The main problem is that guilt feelings may arise from masturbation. Surveys have shown masturbation is a common practice among women as well as men. Some "sexperts," in fact, advocate frequent masturbation to make a person more sensual. Historically, as well as medically, this is not true. (See *Jesus Person Maturity Manual,* David Wilkerson, pp. 53-54 (1971), Regal Books, Glendale, Calif.)

Most churches that have adopted statements regarding masturbation state they "neither condemn nor condone" the practice.

Lynn was an outgoing type who never gave a second thought about speaking to anyone she saw. If a person was friendly, Lynn would strike up a conversation.

One day while visiting her parents Lynn got in a long discussion with the milkman. Her mother was concerned about what the neighbors would think, and rightly so. Mother had heard that the milkman was a real swinger, and she did not want her daughter to find out first hand.

Lynn's friendliness led the milkman to believe Lynn was a goer, and he immediately began pursuing her. Lynn was surprised and shocked. She wondered whatever had put ideas into his head. Lynn needed to learn how to be friendly without appearing flirtatious.

The more common places to look for your Mr. Right are around you wherever you go: your apartment building, church, office, organizations you attend. For some gals this is not an adequate field and they may elect to try computer dating. For some girls computers work, but for others it is apt to be a waste of time and money.

Computer dating often claims to take care of matchmaking. After an interview and one or more tests, all the information about you is fed into the computer. *Voila!* Lists of men's names appear. Some plans even promise a new name every six weeks for three years.

You should be on your way to marital bliss. Or

bigamy!

The fee for this little adventure can run from $10 to $500. Terms vary, but they all promise men. Some may live 2,000 miles away, but love supposedly has no limits.

The computer has been known to match a young man of 21 with a woman of 45. Then there is the case of the 72-year old man who doubted any woman would want him because he was incapable of performing as a husband. The computer matched him up with a middle-aged woman who was tired of over-sexed men.

After their date the computer center received an indignant call from the woman. That dear little man had tried to pull her into bed. Not too incapable after all!

Computer dating may be your kind of thing. I'm inclined to think a sensitive woman wants to know what kind of man she is about to date.

Beforehand.

This is not to exclude blind dates. They are often fun. Usually your friend who lined it up knows you—and him—better than any computer does.

I'd be naive to think that a girl (even a nice one with high standards) falls in love with a man and then lets him do nothing more than walk her to the door and give her a goodnight peck on the cheek.

Roger and Nancy were planning to marry, but the wedding was six months off. They were so much in love. How could they ever wait that long to get their warm bodies close?

The two decided a night in a motel wouldn't be noticed by anyone. Since they were Christians and didn't want to consummate the union before the wedding they decided to "just go to bed and be close."

Unfortunately the wedding was moved up four months. Nancy was pregnant.

A woman can become pregnant without intercourse if the penis brushes against her vaginal opening. The small amount of semen that leaks from the penis during love play can contain as many as 50,000 sperm.

It only takes one. More women than Nancy have learned this—the hard way—through a splash pregnancy.

Another danger in excessive love play (petting, oral sex) is the frustration it causes. Reports show that extensive love play without intercourse can cause psychological problems after marriage. It sometimes accounts for a woman's inability to reach orgasm during normal intercourse.

A man and woman in love can wait for intercourse, but not too long! That is why a mature couple (ready emotionally and financially for marriage) should not plan too long an engagement period.

Pre-marital sex is as wrong for the single woman as adultery is for the married. This is why you, as a sensitive woman, need to cultivate a beautiful sexual life. One that neither you or your huband will desire to flee.

The Bible says divorce is permissible only if adultery has been committed.

If the partner who has committed adultery claims to be a Christian, he has sinned and must seek forgiveness. The partner of this person, as well as God, must forgive (this is difficult for the partner—God is eager to forgive the contrite)!

If God, who created the human body, can forgive—you can too. On the other hand, if the adulterer does not choose to seek forgiveness but desires a divorce, then be willing.

The purpose of holding a marriage together is for

a couple to become more closely united to one another through their Creator.

A further word about reconciliaton: It may seem out of the question but I have known cases where it has happened and the love affair has blossomed.

Poet Miguel Cervantes said, "The worst reconciliation is preferable to the best divorce."

Reconciliation requires maturity, patience, unselfishness, and willingness to learn to be sensitive to each other—but it is possible. Both parties must want it. When dialogue is resumed and a deeper spiritual search is in progress, the fractured marriage has a good chance to knit together firmly.

When reconciliation is not possible, divorce with its adjustments, may be the only alternative.

Some women, whose sex lives prior to divorce had almost evaporated, have already made a sexual adjustment through other activities. For the divorcee who adheres to the Christian standards, continence is the rule.

Recognize these needs and drives—don't repress them. Try to channel them. I have known more than a few women who—though married—have been sexually unfulfilled.

They have tried masturbation and extra-marital affairs. They found momentary release—followed by guilt feelings. Nothing truly satisfied until they developed a personal relationship with God.

Sarah had been divorced two years. She tried every avenue she could think of to find happiness. Loneliness and depression were her worst enemies.

One day after church a friend told her that church attendance alone was not doing a thing for her Christian life. She had to allow a love affair with Christ to take place, the friend said.

Sarah gave herself completely to Christ and willingly allowed God to rule her life. She found—for the first time—a joy that was greater than anything she had ever experienced before or after her marriage breakup.

Sarah discovered Christ could be the trusted Friend she needed to ease her through the troubled waters of living alone.

One of the greatest problems for the formerly married woman is her vulnerability. Many men consider a divorcee fair game. She is sexually experienced and probably hungry for a little excitement, they reason.

Watch out. You can set yourself up for a fall as well as emotional upset.

If you decide to remarry, past experiences may or may not prepare you for a more sound and healthy marital relationship.

You have to be cautious about dating. No matter how great a need you have for sexual fulfillment, intercourse now is not right. Many men, when they find a woman willing to relinquish her body, lose interest in any serious relationship or commitment.

Before you commit yourself to another marriage contract, make sure God is first in your life. Know if your prospective husband shares your beliefs. Know if he is sensitive to your needs and those of your children—if you have any.

More than anything, make sure you can communicate. It takes strong emotional bonds plus maturity and continual renewing of your relationship to preserve a marriage.

These are the requirements on the human side of remarriage. The scale must be balanced with the spiritual requirement. After searching the Scriptures and talking with your pastor, rabbi, or priest, you should know whether marrying again is for you.

Your degree of involvement in the Sexual Revolution is determined by your marital or non-marital status and your personal principles. You call the shots. You have learned and will continue to learn more about your sexuality. As you do, remember that sex can be an enriching experience but your body first belongs to God. What you do with it will be to His glory or shame.

9

LEARNING ABOUT LOVE

There are a number of women in the world today that are not married. Many of the single women are between the ages of 18 and 25. They are the post-World War II babies. They entered a world that was supposed to be free from war. Psychologists were saying children needed to be given more freedom.

No sooner had people adjusted to peace time, than we were invilved in another war. This time in Korea. Children, at a very early age, were learning about war again.

Korea ended and another war began in Viet Nam. The 18-25 group heard nothing but war, war, war. Peace, peace, peace. They have a mission. They have a fear. What will tomorrow bring?

"Eat, drink, and be merry, for tomorrow we may be blown up," some youth say. This philosophy can change all attitudes including those about sex.

Many of the single people believe in any kind of love as long as it doesn't hurt anyone. Others have standards they want to keep.

What should a young single girl do? Several have asked me: "Where do single girls with high standards and morals fit in today's society?"

Single girls between 14 and 24 make up a large

part of the 40 million unattached people in the United States, 19 percent of our population. The number of all singles has increased 47 percent since 1960.

The trend toward later marriages makes it in vogue to be single. Between 1960 and 1971 the number of unmarried females between 18 and 24 increased from 41 percent to 48 percent of the total single population between these ages.

The world is your rainbow. If your single days turn into years, you will find you have the opportunity to bring joy and happiness to many others.

A single life is free of commitments to a spouse. You can pretty much go where and when you wish. Make the most of those years.

If and when the love bug bites, be prepared to make it develop into something wonderful. If you are married see if the following exercise can help you strengthen your love for your husband.

A sensitive woman knows love. She knows how to love her parents, brothers, and sisters. She is acquainted with the type of love she used to have for boyfriends and best girl friends. She knows about the love she possesses for her husband. But, does she know about Agape?

We have but one multipurpose word in English that must stand for four Greek words meaning love.

Do the following exercise on love. You may have to do some deep thinking, but be honest:

Set I
1. How did you feel as a child when you sat on your mother's lap?
2. Do you still have the same basic feeling toward your parents or other relatives?
3. Who did you run to when you were frightened?
4. If you have children, why do you do without something in order for your child to have his

heart's desire?

Set II
1. How did you feel as a child when you made out your first party invitation list?
2. What were your feelings when you said, "My best friend . . ."?
3. Are you still close with those same individuals?

Set III
1. As a teen did you have a new feeling inside you as you looked at that handsome boy across the room?
2. What about the first time a boy kissed you? How did you feel?
3. Did you ever see a movie and then dream about the hero making love to you?

Set IV
1. Do you give yourself because of obligation or love?
2. Do you forgive the person who has done you wrong?
3. After a period of conflict are you able to see your faults?

Glance over each set of questions. The four sets represent one of the forms of love defined by the Greeks? Can you match the Greek word with the correct set?

"Storge" is your first love affair. It is the need each individual has to be loved and cared for—your mother's lap to sit on or the helping hand of dad. Those gifts—big and small—tried to express love—yet the real love was deep within your heart.

"Philia" is a sincere love between good friends, but is generally temporary. This love is not meant to endure.

Women are at first made aware of their feelings for a man through "eros" love. Eros includes those tingly feelings, the palpitations of the heart, the immediacy of contact—to speak, touch, or just see at closer range.

We begin to experience eros in the teen years. It is the love that initiates a relationship with a future mate. The development of this love into "agape" depends on your relationship to God— your discernment and sensitivity—along with communication with your mate. It is the "in spite of" kind of love. Agape does not necessarily begin with eros. I have known happy couples where there were no heart palpitations and tingly feelings. They had a calm, sincere love that was beautiful.

"Agape," the highest of all love, is the beginning of eternal life through Jesus Christ. We could not begin to comprehend agape it we did not understand the other three types of love.

Unfortunately many people (could you be one?) have never experienced the sheer grace of agape. Through the Love that Jesus can place in your heart (God is love), you can know the joy of all four dimensions of love.

As a man and woman fall in love and form a contract under God, it is their responsibility to follow His will.

When the Pharisees came to Jesus to test His authority they asked, "Is it lawful to divorce one's wife for any cause?"

Jesus answered: "Have you not read that he who made them from the beginning made them male and female, and said, 'For this reason a man shall leave his father and mother and be joined to his wife, and the two shall become one'? So they are no longer two but one. Whom therefore God has joined, let no man put asunder."

There is a third party—God. So it is not *your* will. Or your husband's will.

You are one, united under God. You are to follow *His* will.

It may be easier to talk about divorce than to see each other face to face, but if God is the third party and you know your marriage is His will, then you shall overcome.

It is a good prescription to read the wedding vows over periodically.

Some women very dear to me have had to face the dilemma of divorce. They agree that if their pastor had been more explicit and if they had been more mature in their early months and years of marriage, the wedge would not have developed. Married love takes time to mature. It cannot grow apart from God.

A number of couples forget the Bible as a source-book for love. Often during the early years of marriage—and occasionally now—my husband and I read I Corinthians 13 aloud together after a misunderstanding or when our love became resentful or touchy. We were so sure of the truth in this chapter that we had the reference engraved inside our wedding bands. It is a constant reminder of agape love—the love that God wants us to share.

When we have a misunderstanding, one is more at fault than the other, but we never need to rub it in. We have become sensitive to our faults and our guilt feelings. It is difficult to read this biblical passage together because it is painful. It reveals truth in our lives.

Once we do, the wounds heal immediately. They never have a chance to fester. Some of the most difficult words in the English language are "I'm sorry" and "forgive me." Every marriage needs these words.

To keep your love relationship growing adopt I Corinthians 13 as the prescription for your marriage. I've never known it to fail.

10

VARIETY ADDS SPICE TO YOUR LIFE

We women enjoy learning the latest sewing techniques and trying out new recipes. When it comes to sex, it also seems we just cannot get suggestions fast enough (witness the landslide sale of popular books that tell you everything you have ever wanted to know—and more—about the subject of sex, the art of married love, what women should and shouldn't do to attract men).

I believe in creativity. And experimentation. Too many marriages end in bedroom boredom because the man or the woman—or both—lack imagination and zest.

Some couples are like the man who goes into the fifty-flavor ice cream parlor and always orders one scoop of vanilla.

No variety. Perhaps you cannot expect most folks to enjoy all fifty flavors, but pity the soul who will not venture beyond the standard brand.

Some of the sexual techniques that you read about that have been enjoyable to other couples may—or may not—appeal to you. One thing about it—you will never know if you don't try.

When you think of love play what comes to your mind? Do you enjoy having certain areas petted?

Have you ever thought that your husband has the same feelings? If you do not know what thrills your man, do some exploring; you need to start learning. The adventure is fun.

Trial and error is one way to learn what pleases your lover, but inquiry is the fastest. Ask: "What would feel good to you?"

Think of your husband as an extension of yourself. Remember that he receives many of the same sensations in his erogenous zones that you do in yours. Communication works wonders, and when you begin to please him he is likely to respond in full measure—to your pleasure as well. You have been united through the bond of marriage. The privileges of sexual expression are yours. Now make something of it! Give of your physical, mental, and emotional self.

We live in a world all wrapped up in the liberated woman. I am liberated as a woman. At the same time I am united with my husband. We are individuals, yet one in spirit.

I support him in his endeavors. He is interested in my experiences at home, my tutoring (I teach reading), my activities in women's organizations. We share our thoughts, feelings, likes and dislikes.

Most of all, we share ourselves.

I am speaking to you as a married woman, but whatever your marital status, pre-marital or extra-marital affairs violate the laws of God, and tend to bring frustration and unhappiness. If you are married, you will more likely not be as tempted to have affairs if you spend your efforts concentrating on building a satisfying sexual relationship with your husband.

If you are single your temptations may be harder to fight, but a happy life is more certain if you remain true to your convictions to abstain from pre-marital relationships. You will be ahead of most singles if you remember that the secret of an intense love affair is dialogue with your lover and a personal relationship to God.

An Exercise to Do: If you are married, think for a moment about your husband. He is your man. Can you tell some quality of his that you admire in him? What three things did he do during the past week that made you the happiest? Draw a long line on a piece of paper. Draw perpendicular lines at each end and in the center of the line you just drew. Divide each half of the line into degrees between the center and end by drawing short lines that intersect the long line. Mark the left end of your scale "Never Ned." Mark the right end of your scale "Always-ready Albert." Mark the center of your scale "Just-right Jeremy." Where on this scale would you rate your husband as a lover today? Draw a line at that point on your scale.

Your honeymoon was ecstasy. Gradually, however, your sex life may have settled down to earth. Maybe it is even partly buried. Who is at fault if sex for you two is not anything to boast about? What four approaches could you try to change your husband's rating on your scale? Begin at once.

Make sure to use every idea and method you know to turn your man on. You must be proud of what you have and what you can give your man. There is no room for selfishness in a dynamic marriage and love affair. (I'm not talking about two separate encounters; marriage should be a continuing love affair.)

Do not let your relations be "wham, bam, thank you, ma'm." Lovemaking demands intensity, expression, intimacy, and orgasm. Do not settle for anything less.

Of course there will be times when the moment

of passion is less than perfect. Do not fret. Think about the next time. Your emotional makeup has a lot to do with your initiative and response. A mediocre intimacy should not cause you to withdraw or be inhibited.

Cuddle your man. In some ways he is like a child. His face may be rough and his hands calloused but every man needs to be treated tenderly.

Alice grew up with the notion that the man was to make love to the woman—never the other way around. She had always been passive during love play.

After being convinced that it really was all right for a woman to caress a man, she said: "It was like a whole new world. I found that we were making love. I had become an instrument. Now that I know he desires and needs to be petted we are like an orchestra—the sounds blend. There are crescendos. It's wonderful!"

Do not let your husband's ego slip. Do not let him feel inferior or unwanted. Tell him how thankful you are that he is the head of the house. And your husband. Compliment him (if it can be genuine) on his thoughtful qualities. Let him know in what ways he excels as a lover. Verbally praise him.

If you practice the sensitivity exercises and become aware of your man's needs and drives, you will give him all the excitement he will want. The techniques you use are between you and your man. You should become as uninhibited as necessary to please him. This is very important to harmonious relations.

How can you become an expert in sexual techniques? First, be sensitive. Notice any difference in your attitude yet? More important, has your husband? Maybe he has noticed a little difference. After this chapter you should wow him.

The second requirement for perfecting sex techniques is the willingness to experiment. "But how?" I can hear some of you say.

Women are either ready to experiment or they are too inhibited. You have already decided to become a more sensuous woman. You have read more than half the book. Do not stop now.

Some women have become conditioned not to talk—even to their husbands—about such things as sex-fondling, intercourse positions, and other sex-related topics. Once you and your husband do begin to discuss these matters creatively there is mutual benefit.

Oral love play—using the lips, mouth, and tongue to stimulate a partner's sexual organs—is a common practice; perhaps some 70 to 80 percent of all couples engage in it at least periodically.

Frequently men and women feel a bed is the only place for love play. To be sure, a bed is the most common place, but it is far from the only one.

An Exercise to Do: On a cold winter night when you have had a roaring fire in the fireplace, don one of your outfits from the *Passion Pack* while your man is showering. Grab a fluffy quilt, spread it in front of the fireplace, light some candles, and wait patiently.

When you are not in bed, he will call for you or come wandering out.

You will respond:

"I'm by the fire. Come here a moment."

If you have on background music it will fade into the distance as your man gets closer and closer. . . .

A word of caution: Make sure the children do not come barging in on your fireplace affair.

Children can be a definite obstacle. On an evening when the children are to be at a friend's house, plan to have an early dinner and a time for two.

Allow yourselves a long period of love play. You will be amazed at how relaxed you can be.

This is a good opportunity to share verbally your thoughts about love play. You do not have to worry about whispering or being overheard.

Visually stimulate your lover.

Let him chase you from room to room. Tease him. Show him you can play games.

Many husbands of mothers with small children see only their wives' tired, tempered moments. Your man will be surprised to see you frisky, fresh, and fancy. Your marriage will thrive like a parched petunia after a summer shower.

Speaking of showers, we know a couple that enjoys taking one together in a friend's oversized shower. They think it is a rare treat.

Making love in the shower may sound all wet to you, but don't knock it if you haven't tried it.

Some swear by swimming pools on a moonlight night to keep their love bouyant. Caution: underwater stunts may be hazardous to your health.

A friend has a secret desire to have large mirrors surrounding a canopy bed. Her husband would love to have an obstetrician's table so that he could love his wife more adequately. He sees her as a doll to be cherished and he wants to please her fully without causing her discomfort.

While these techniques—or sexual aids—may seem far out, they are perfectly normal to creative couples.

Maybe your husband is the kind who won't budge when a game is on television. If so, do not nag him about it! Remind him about the game (it shows your interest and support). Serve him little tidbits to eat.

Then go take a bath, put on a transparent gown and dab a little perfume. Do your nails or something until the game is over, then casually walk in front of the TV and sit suggestively (but discreetly) on the sofa.

If he is really hard-nosed, rub his neck, kiss his ear.

Any time you kiss your husband, be relaxed. Do not tighten up your lips like you have a case of lockjaw. Let your lips melt together as you yield yourself to him.

Not long ago a young girl asked me if it was okay for a good girl to wiggle her hips. Yes, if she is enticing her husband. Men like to see hips move. Let your husband see yours—not those of the burlesque bawdies in the bump-and-grind shows.

For the couple that enjoy the outdoors there is "love in the lupine." Lupine is a delicate plant with white, yellow, or (most commonly) purple flowers that grows in mountainous areas.

A romantic moment is to lie down beneath a tree on a fragrant bed of these little flowers. More than one couple I've known have discovered the refreshment this brings after a long day on the trails.

If lupine is not available you can always substitute honeysuckle or some other fragrant and soft foliage. Watch out for stinging nettles and poison oak! Or your love play may come to a sad end!

The great outdoors is a wonderful place to share your love, but the biggest problem is privacy. I've witnessed couples on the beaches, park lawns, and hillsides treating sex too lightly. That kind of display cheapens sex. It is meant to be something special between husband and wife—not shared with the public.

One non-physical sexual technique is to do little things to make your husband think about you when he is out of town.

Remind him of you in little ways: put sexy notes

in the pockets of his pajamas or shirts; hide candy kisses in socks, shoes, clothing or his shaving kit; write notes, one to be read each day he is away.

These simple acts will not physically satisfy his sexual appetite. But if he has had love play prior to his trip and knows you will be waiting with a sexy surprise when he returns, he will tend to his business while he is away.

*   *   *

I have given you a few examples of sex techniques so you can see how beautiful love play can be. The depth of love you experience in your sex life will be determined by your relationship to your mate and to your God.

You are developing sensitivity. You are becoming more sexy.

An Exercise to Do: After you have spent two weeks applying creativity to your love life, rate your husband again on the scale you used in the earlier exercise. Incredible! Right?

11

SENSITIVITY GROWS AND EXPANDS

Sensitive Woman (almost), you are now ready for continuing the exercises to refine your newly developing awareness.

When thinking about love play, view it as a three-act drama. The prologue is the time of preparation. The play itself is the act of intercourse and orgasm. The epilogue is the period of relaxation and afterglow.

Because love play needs to be spontaneous, I hate to prescribe any set techniques or exercises. A few suggestions, though, may help you overcome some common hang-ups. I assure you every married woman faces sexual adjustments.

The prologue of love play can be an instantaneous surge of passion, or it may begin in the morning and culminate late that evening. A sensitive man knows that his wife usually needs to be prepared if she is to totally enjoy their sexual encounter. Do not overlook the fact that many men need the same treatment. Part of the fun is in the preparation.

Preparation can be done through words, actions, a little gift, doing things together. A general expression of love. Seeking together a deeper love relationship is the ideal toward which all couples should strive. Full satisfaction is achieved when husband and wife seek sexual success together.

When you begin the prologue to passion prepare your body the way your husband desires it. (If you don't know—ask him.) Your man may not care how you smell or look, or maybe some one thing—a black negligee, eye makeup, you on a satin sheet—really drives him wild with passion. A friend expressed her thoughts about the role of hygiene in love play this way:

"Ben is generally most appealing to me sexually when he has freshly showered, though we have actually had some of our best times on sticky, hot, midday love fests. I found it surprising to discover that body odors I consider offensive on myself are pleasing, even arousing, to Ben, and he does not like perfume."

I think most men like their woman to smell freshly scrubbed—with or without perfume. Use your judgment about this because you want to please and are sensitive.

Also, you and your lover should decide the best place for engaging in love play and intercourse. Share with your man about the things that distract you—a radio or TV playing, body odors, fear of children coming into the room, the temperature of the room, light or lack of it. Learn what distracts your husband. Eliminate those distractions; you will be pleased when you discover what it does to help you both give your attention to what you plan to enjoy together.

Choose a place that is secure for your love scene. Make sure the walls are not paper thin and the bed does not creak. How about a lock on the door and separate room for the children? Children in the bedroom, even infants, can keep you from reaching orgasm.

Make sure your husband knows that you need to be caressed and aroused before coitus. Take time to express your love verbally and through tender little physical acts.

There should be no set pattern; be spontaneous.

Since I've already discussed attire, I only need to add that if it bothers you to take off all your garments during love play, talk this over with your husband so he isn't wondering what your hang-up is. Some women feel that unless the room is totally dark their sex organs should not be exposed.

A man loves to see the curves of his wife's body. This is thrilling to him. Before you decide to keep something on next time think about what he might like to see.

The prologue is the time to kiss, caress, and embrace. Excitement builds until your husband's penis is rigid and your vagina is moist. Relax.

Intercourse can be painful for the woman—and unpleasant for the man—if the vagina isn't adequately prepared.

If your lover's ejaculaton seems near, hold your caresses for a moment. Some wives complain about early ejaculation. With your cooperation and verbal expression he will be able to hold back until you have had adequate stimulation to match his readiness for intercourse.

The play has been introduced. The drama continues. Excitement builds. You are ready to unite.

Positions for intercourse are many and varied. Your creativity and desires will lead you to the greatest satisfactions.

Rhythmical body movements will intensify the union and add greater sensations. Prolong the act as long as desired.

Holding still and getting your husband's mind on something other than ejaculation will prolong the enjoyment. Avoid strong or jerky movements unless you are both ready for a final thrusting motion.

If the penis is not sufficiently hard and you are ready for orgasm, place your hand just above the base of the penis. Firmly rub the pubic area and verbally express sexual thoughts.

In his book, *Better Is Your Love Than Wine*, (Inter-Varsity Press, page 34, used by permission) Jean Banyolak says, "Marriage is not a destination, it is a journey."

Developing a beautiful sex life is part of that journey.

The epilogue is the time to be consciously aware of your unity.

If you need to be caressed, tell your husband don't make him guess. He may be exhausted. If he wants to sleep, this is no sign he is rejecting you. It is a natural male response.

If he is sensitive to you, he will make an effort to meet your needs by holding you close. Just as it took you longer to be ready for orgasm, your passion subsides more slowly.

Some women have difficulty reaching orgasm. Don't let this frustrate you. Enjoy the union you share. If the problem persists, discuss the matter with your gynecologist.

An Exercise to Do: Sensitivity improves with practice. So does love making. Plan a weekend retreat for the two of you. Find someone to care for the children if you need to do so, then sneak off to a resort motel, on a camping trip, to the city, or wherever the two of you would enjoy.

Be daring! Eat food you have not tried before. Choose activities you have not tried and savor the experiences. Most of all—enjoy each other and your developing sensitivity.

Prayer Helps

Many a woman thirsts for deeper meaning in her life. Maybe that is one reason you are reading this book. You should be more sensitive now than when you began to read, but the ultimate sensitivity comes from the same Source that brought you into being. As a car with defects is returned to the factory, so you can seek your Creator for further growth and development.

An Exercise to Do: This next exercise should sensitize your heart. All I want you to do is pray. Quietly and silently bow your head. Thank God for being there. Ask Him to help you in your quest for sensitivity and to show you how to improve your communication with and sensitivity to Him.

I get excited talking to women about prayer. Any woman who earnestly tries prayer will find her life changed. For the first time she will see that Christ is not a mere historical figure. He is a Man for all seasons.

This love affair blossoms. It spreads to others. Frequently it radiates to a woman's lover if he has not already begun a walk with the Lord.

An Exercise to Do: Read one of the recent books on conversational prayer. Note the free and flowing personal style in which some people communicate with God. In your prayer relationship to God you may choose to be informal rather than formal if that style of communication suits you and helps you feel God's presence.

Most women know something about prayer. Frequent and fervent prayer is foreign to many, however. We have looked briefly at how we can develop a deeper communication with God. Now we need to see why it should become a way of life.

Some women only pray for a very sick child or a dying parent. My husband calls such intercession "parachute prayers"—excellent to have available in an emergency situation. God surely hears and respects the request.

A prayer problem for some people is that they do not feel close enough to God to be completely honest. If in the past you talked to God only when you had no other place to turn, maybe you need to develop a regular time of prayer.

God knows your concerns. He wants you to humble yourself and seek His help daily—not just in times of emergency only.

I often hear women say, "Oh, God . . ." There is a distinct tone of disrespect in such useage and lack of knowledge of the Person about whom they are talking. What are the chances God will comfort such women when needs must be met? Probably slim, if their frivolous use of His name truly shows their lack of knowledge about God. God can comfort only if there is respect and a desire to know and seek him.

On the surface, many women say they want a deeper prayer life. What they need to achieve is a regular prayer life.

Women are buying books on prayer, joining prayer circles, and talking about prayer, yet they just cannot seem to give God fifteen uninterrupted minutes in a day.

It is not easy. I know. I fight the daily battle of the clock and interruptions myself.

Give prayer a chance. Make up your mind to be persistent. If being alone, talking to God, is difficult, begin by spending two minutes a day in prayer. Increase it until you get to fifteen minutes.

A life with Christ as an occasional guest is nice, but when He becomes a member of the household, your life takes on a new dimension.

A couple desiring a baby can read the books on

child care and obtain all the physical necessities to equip an infant nursery, but not until they hold the baby in their arms and care for it do they truly know what parenthood is. Parenthood must be experienced.

It is the same with prayer.

"Great!" you say. "I'll start a regular prayer life and everything will be fine."

Wait! I never said that. Prayer is a way of life, a road that takes you to the Father. God never promised a superhighway to Heaven. . . . There are many turns and ruts. The journey to Heaven takes time, but with a determined vehicle you will make it. And the rewards are great.

The Christian life may be compared to a fruit tree. Christ is the trunk; you are the branches. If a tree is to be fruitful it must be watered, fertilized, and pruned. We must be fed through Scripture, committed to Christ daily, and willing to be used and disciplined. We must share our faith (Read John 15 in the Bible.)

One reason that the Jesus People have gained such wide attention is because they live what they believe. They share what they feel. "Jesus loves you," they say, and they want the whole world to know.

They are tired of the established church talking about Christianity and then bickering over doctrinal and organizational matters.

Christianity is commitment to Christ and life based on His teachings.

Do not be discouraged if you are tempted, tried, or tormented. The Christian life is not easy. It takes a person willing to stand up and be counted. One who has strength of character.

Christianity is not for conformists.

Continue your exercise in prayer now: Take the

time you have allotted for prayer and divide it into five sections. If you want to begin on a small scale, start with two and one-half minutes. Give thirty seconds to each of the following: adoration, confession, thanksgiving, and supplication—intercession and petition.

You may find thirty seconds just is not enough for each topic. Keep your mind on the prayer, not on the clock.

Adoration

In adoration you are coming to your Father with praise. We are familiar with "Our Father, which art in heaven, hallowed by thy name" (Luke 11:2). We address God as the eternal King, immortal, all-powerful. This is a time to say—in our own way— "I love You, God."

Few women feel they can honestly say they love God because they do not know Him that well. Love between you and God will grow as it should between you and your lover. After all, God is love.

Through adoration an immediate contact is made with God. It is from adoration that all sincere prayer springs.

Confession

Confession—good for the soul—is indispensable for the Christian. We need to tell God we are sorry for what we have done wrong. Likewise, we need to seek forgiveness for our sins of omission—what we have left undone.

Remember, there are sins of the flesh like adultery, gluttony, stealing, drunkenness. And sins of the spirit, such as jealousy, envy, greed, and hate— to mention only a few. We all have plenty for which to seek God's forgiveness.

Thanksgiving

Many of us are familiar with the prayer of thanksgiving. I think many women offer their first real prayer of gratitude at the birth of their child (or at the reception of an adopted one).

There is something about parenthood that makes a mother want to give thanks. There are other times for thanksgiving too.

You can sum up all the good things in your life, place them before God, and express your thanks.

It may seem contradictory, but you should also use this part of your prayer to accept your adversities. Naturally you are not happy about everything that has happened to you.

Still, if you have put yourself in God's hands, you should accept it as part of His plan. Be thankful that He is in control, and be willing to accept His will in all things.

Intercession

Supplication or intercession is prayer for others. It is the time you bring the needs and blessings of your friends and family before God.

I find it helps to keep a little notebook with the names of friends and their specific needs listed inside.

On our kitchen bulletin board are pinned the pictures of family, friends, and missionary acquaintances. The photos are a daily reminder of those far away. We may not always know their special needs, but we are aware of them as persons and of their need for prayer.

Petition

The last form of prayer is petition. This is prayer for one's self. I have heard it said: "God first, others second, and yourself third." This is the right order for prayer.

God instructs us in His Word to bring our needs and concerns to Him. Just as a child tells his parents about his need for new shoes, so we can petition our Heavenly Father for our needs and wants.

There is a simple way to remember the ingredients of prayer: Adoration, Confession, Thanksgiving and Supplication—the first letter of each spells ACTS. Our prayers bring about acts and action. Remember that word when you begin prayer. After praying through each of the letters, add your own requests to God.

You will have a well-rounded prayer time.

Expect a new relationship to God. Expect great things. Let your prayer life develop into a dialogue. Take a few moments after prayer to sit, stand, or kneel in quiet. You can come to know what it means to say, "I felt God speaking to me today."

12

SENSITIVITY IS WORTH IT ALL

We have all heard about love triangles. I'm going to tell you about one that will stick in your mind for a long time. It will if you are serious about being a sensitive woman.

Remember in the beginning of the book when I was speaking about the garden of Eden? We women have come a long way (as they say) since then—literally and figuratively.

Woman was beautiful, delightful, precious, and pure, but she allowed the cunning words of an evil creature to take away her innocence. We, the descendants of this woman, have continually tried to change. We have found it impossible—except through a new life.

In chapter 3 we learned how to practice using the senses, how to see ourselves from the inside. In the latter part of chapter 11 we learned how to meet the one Person who, through His Spirit, can fulfill us completely.

You are God's creation. God's gift to you is the Holy Spirit. He has promised never to leave you desolate. Through Jesus Christ, who promised the gift of the Spirit, you can have a new life.

An abundant one.

God created Man and Woman and bestowed love upon them. It was made manifest through Jesus Christ. Because of love (storge, philia, eros and agape) we are able to reach out in love to others. We have the resources in Christ to love all men if we are sensitive to them.

We are free to decide what our relationship to God will be. He is society's most permissive parent. To those who yield to Him, desirous of a more abundant life, He is the greatest disciplinarian. His Spirit is the taskmaster.

A yielded child knows when he is alienated from his Heavenly Father. Remember Woman in the garden? She realized her alienation. She was embarrassed and scared. She and Man covered their nakedness and tried to hide. It is uncomfortable to be in such a predicament.

On the other hand, Woman was given free will. Even though she made the wrong decision God is willing for her descendants to be redeemed through His Son.

Earlier I referred to the sensation of thirst as a reminder of the physical needs of our neighbors.

John, in his Gospel, points out an interesting parallel between physical and spiritual thirst. He recounts the story of an encounter between Jesus and a Samaritan woman at a countryside well.

Jesus, tired from a long journey, sat down about noontime beside the well (John 4:5-30). Before long a Samaritan woman came to draw out some water.

"Please give me a drink," Jesus asked her.

The request was unheard of because the Jews and the Samaritans were not on speaking terms.

The conversation continued, the surprised woman talking about physical thirst, Jesus using the encounter to sensitize her to spiritual thirst, and how to quench it.

She satisfied His physical thirst. But Jesus said: "Everyone who drinks this water will be thirsty again. But whoever drinks the water I will give him will never be thirsty again. For my gift will become a spring in the man himself, welling up into eternal life" (John 4:13, 14. Phillips, J. B. *The New Testament in Modern English*).

The Samaritan woman wanted *that* kind of water —"so that I may stop being thirsty," she said.

Jesus satisfied her spiritual thirst, that sex with five husbands—and another man who was not her husband at all—could not satisfy.

Christ alone gives the water of eternal life that quenches the thirsty soul and brings meaning to the physical union between husband and wife.

God instituted marriage because he saw man's need for companionship, procreation, and physical pleasure.

Here is our love triangle: God, self, sex.

It's easy to see how God and self are related, and how self and sex go together. It is harder to perceive the relationship between God and sex.

We have seen that anatomical sex was created in the garden by God. He saw that Man needed a helpmeet to share life with him. God gave Woman the body that is admired by Man. Thus sex is the good gift of God to Man and Woman.

Sex, as created by God, is sacramental.

So be sexy, sensual, and spiritual. Remember that each makes *sense* only through God in Jesus Christ.

Before Russ and I were married we decided to put Christ first in every realm of our married life. After our wedding and the festive reception we drove to the Beverly Hilton Hotel near Los Angeles. We unloaded our suitcases (after having to cut apart the ropes that the best man and the maid of

honor had used to tie all our luggage together—
their little joke), checked into the hotel, and prepared to retire.

Many couples, I think, simply jump into bed on
their wedding night.

As Christians, Russ and I had often discussed our
marriage expectations. We had often ended our
dates with prayer.

When the big moment came at the Hilton, Russ
knelt beside the bed. He asked me to join him.
Together we came before God, seeking His blessing
on our marriage.

(Now before you get the idea that we are super-
pious, let me set you straight. We don't always
preface sex with bedside devotions. Sometimes we
pray before or after and sometimes we don't.
Sometimes we simply jump into bed.)

That first night we read aloud I Corinthians 13,
the great chapter on love. We thanked God for our
families who had given us the wedding, for the
beautiful ceremony, and for each other. We asked
God to be present in every part of our marriage—
to help us be sensitive to each other. We asked God
to use us according to His will. Then we closed
with the Lord's Prayer.

After that time on our knees before God we con-
summated our marriage. That was the beginning of
a beautiful love affair.

Sex without God can be selfish. Physical sex alone
often diminishes through the years. In a marriage
with God at the center, sex not only endures. . . .

It gets better and better.

BOOKS FOR MORE READING

The mere fact that a book is listed in the bibliography below is not intended to be construed as total endorsement of the book's contents. Readers may find themselves exposed to some ideas in which they are in total disagreement. The discriminate reader will be able to select the content that can contribute to her spiritual quest for sensitivity and to reject what is non-essential.

Augsberger, David. 1970. *Be All You Can Be*. Carol Stream, Ill.: Creation House.

Banyolak, Jean. 1971. *Better Is Your Love Than Wine*. Downers Grove, Ill.: Inter-Varsity Press.

Bovet, Theodor. 1958. *A Handbook to Marriage*. Garden City, N.Y.: Dolphin Books, Doubleday & Co., Inc.

Hefley, James C. 1971. *Sex Sense and Nonsense*. Elgin, Ill.: David C. Cook Publishing Co. Order number 56135.

Lindsell, Harold. 1969. *When You Pray*. Wheaton, Ill.: Tyndale House.

Mace, David R. *Marriage: The Art of Lasting Love*. Garden City, N. Y.: Doubleday & Co., Inc.

Mace, David R. 1953. *Whom God Hath Joined*. Philadelphia: Westminster Press.

Miles, Herbert J. 1967. *Sexual Happiness in Marriage*. Grand Rapids, Mich.: Zondervan.

Parker, William, and St. Johns, Elaine. 1957. *Prayer Can Change Your Life*. Englewood Cliffs, N. J.: Prentice-Hall, Inc.

Peterson, J. Allan (ed.). 1971. *The Marriage Affair*. Wheaton, Ill.: Tyndale House.

Phillips, J. B. 1958. *The New Testament in Modern English*. New York City: The Macmillan Company.

Shedd, Charlie W. 1965. *Letters to Karen*. Nashville: Abingdon Press.

Shedd, Charlie W. 1968. *Letters to Philip*. Old Tappan, N. J.: Spire Books, Fleming Revell Co.

Tournier, Paul. 1962. *To Understand Each Other*. Richmond, Va.: John Knox Press.

Winter, Gibson. 1961. *Love and Conflict*. Garden City, N. Y.: Dolphin Books, Doubleday & Co.

Notes